More Praise for

STRONGER

"This is an unusual book from a talented author that's well worth reading for those interested in growing their business. Twenty-five years ago, Dr. Strouse and I co-founded the www.ceoclubs. org, a worldwide association of CEOs. Since then I have written 27 books that have sold several million copies—and what I don't tell everyone is that a good many of my ideas came from this talented writer/speaker/friend. I suggest you buy his book *Stronger* to develop the resilience you need to succeed."

—Joe Mancuso, Co-founder, www.ceoclubs.org

"This is much more than a guide for attaining individual success. . . . To have adequate standards of well-being, we must now begin to build a resilient society as well. This book invaluably points the way to achieving both personal and societal resilience."

—Cathal Flynn, retired Rear Admiral,
US Navy, and former SEAL

STRONGER

DEVELOP *the* RESILIENCE YOU NEED *to* SUCCEED

George S. Everly Jr., Ph.D.

Douglas A. Strouse, Ph.D.

Dennis K. McCormack, Ph.D.

AMERICAN MANAGEMENT ASSOCIATION

New York · Atlanta · Brussels · Chicago · Mexico City · San Francisco
Shanghai · Tokyo · Toronto · Washington, D.C.

This publication is designed to provide accurate and authoritative information in regard to the subject matter covered. It is sold with the understanding that the publisher is not engaged in rendering legal, accounting, or other professional service. If legal advice or other expert assistance is required, the services of a competent professional person should be sought.

LIBRARY OF CONGRESS CATALOGING-IN-PUBLICATION DATA
Everly, George S., Jr., 1950-
Stronger : develop the resilience you need to succeed / George S. Everly, Jr., Ph.D., Douglas A. Strouse, Ph.D., Dennis K. McCormack, Ph.D.
pages cm
Includes bibliographical references and index.
ISBN 978-0-8144-3604-2 (hardcover : alk. paper) -- ISBN 978-0-8144-3605-9 (ebook) 1. Resilience (Personality trait) 2. Success. I. Strouse, Douglas A. II. McCormack, Dennis K. III. Title.
BF698.35.R47E94 2015
650.1--dc23   2015009467

About AMA
American Management Association (www.amanet.org) is a world leader in talent development, advancing the skills of individuals to drive business success. Our mission is to support the goals of individuals and organizations through a complete range of products and services, including classroom and virtual seminars, webcasts, webinars, podcasts, conferences, corporate and government solutions, business books, and research. AMA's approach to improving performance combines experiential learning—learning through doing—with opportunities for ongoing professional growth at every step of one's career journey.

Printing number
10 9 8 7 6 5 4 3 2 1

To Patti Copps. Kind and loving. Courageous and tenacious. You are as beautiful inside as you are outside. You are truly STRONGER! And to my grandchildren, Olivia and Bentley. May you know only happiness, but just in case . . . *read this book*!! GSE

To my family, where I saw and learned the dimensions and power of resiliency; my wife and loving partner, Sharon Toher Strouse; my children, Kimberly, Kevin, and Kristin (who lives with us in spirit); my sisters, Rosalie and Gale; and my brothers, James and Charles. DAS

To my wife, Michelle, my ongoing source of strength for my accomplishments, and to all who strive to better themselves when dealing with adversity. DKM

CONTENTS

FOREWORD

Stronger is a most compelling study of human behavior and the ability to successfully cope with adversity and all of its ramifications. The authors believe that resilience may be defined as the ability to adapt to or rebound from adversity, a trait that has had an impact on me personally and to a great degree on my chosen professional military career as a naval officer with assignments on ships, staffs in the Pentagon, Vietnam, Germany, and, operationally, as a member of the Navy's Underwater Demolition and SEAL Teams.

The authors are interested in how people adjust to adversity and what the core factors are that allow them to survive and prosper in what can be very trying times. They cite five such core factors to achieving personal resilience, what they call "psychological body armor": active optimism, decisive action, moral compass, relentless tenacity, and interpersonal support.

Optimism heads the list. Cynics need not apply, because the cynic is always content with the way things are, or that there is no better option for rectifying a situation. Often disguised as humor, cynicism tries punching holes in optimistic emotion. It never gets started. Optimism defines the limits of potential outcomes and will be fairly stated by the persistent optimist. Indeed, optimism is a necessary element to enlightened leadership.

Decisive action, not file fumbling, is the hallmark of an energized organization. Get around the table and study an issue as long as needed; ensure group buy-in to the several courses of action; decide on it; and step out. Case closed, but ready for potential road bumps. Develop resilience, which will naturally evolve out of determination and persistence.

Moral compass. The West Point motto is "Duty, Honor, Country." This works well in combat and our wars. It will work well in a commercial enterprise and is bedrock to ethical behavior.

Relentless tenacity. Pay attention to detail and singleness of purpose. Put teeth into tenacity. To see adversity through requires tenacity.

Interpersonal support is a team sport. In Special Operations Forces there is a constant recognition that their missions most likely require outside backup, airlifts, ships, logistics, etc. Actions in war require teamwork in order to be successful, just like in any organization. A smoothly functioning organization draws its strength from robust interpersonal support. The resilient leader recognizes this in his team.

These five factors of personal resilience are keys to improving work habits and output. They are indispensable at all levels of human endeavor. We all wonder how we will survive the inevitable bad news that sometimes accompanies our existence. Handling the unannounced news can be a systemic shock. Having the necessary resilience is key to survival.

Stronger is a powerful read that takes us on a journey to successfully navigate the maze of dealing with personal and professional adversity.

George R. Worthington, Rear Admiral, USN (SEAL), retired
Former Assistant Secretary of Defense for Special Operations
Former Commander, Naval Special Warfare Command
San Diego, California

PREFACE

What do baseball great Cal Ripken Jr., neurosurgeon Ben Carson, Governor Martin O'Malley, accident survivor Pat Rummerfield, Olympic champion Jim Craig, psychologist Abbey-Robin Tillery, and U.S. Navy SEAL Moki Martin all have in common? They have what we believe is the single most powerful factor that will help you realize your full potential, that will foster your happiness, and that will assist you in achieving both your personal and professional goals in life. They have personal resilience—or what we sometimes refer to as psychological body armor.

In 1989, the movie *Indiana Jones and the Last Crusade* was released. The popular fictional movie starring Harrison Ford and Sean Connery told the story of a death-defying quest for the Holy Grail. The Grail was a treasure prized above all things because, according to legend, those who drank from it would be granted immortality. Many pursued the Grail, but even the movie's heroes were unable to take it from the boundaries of its resting place.

In the same year, another death-defying quest was undertaken. This wasn't a fictional pursuit of immortality but a real-life quest for something that many have unsuccessfully pursued: immunity to excessive stress. More specifically, this was a quest to discover how one might resist, or rebound from, disease-causing stress and the potentially disabling consequences of aversive life experiences. Unlike the movie, this immunity doesn't have boundaries. Millions around the globe can benefit from this form of human resilience that we call psychological body armor. While physical body armor worn by police and military personnel protects against physical injury, psychological body armor is designed to protect us from potentially stifling and even disabling adversity. And while there are several components that constitute a full suit of physical body armor, there are also, we believe, several that constitute a full suit of psychological body armor.

Our quest for this type of resilience started not with a treasure map but with something much more interesting: the creation of virtual-reality models of health and disease. In collaboration with Kenneth Smith, a gifted statistician and professor and chairman of accounting and legal studies at Salisbury University, we were interested in creating virtual-reality models documenting the pathogenic forces of a psychologically toxic workplace. To do this we used statistical models designed to depict relationships of cause and effect.

To our surprise, we found that what caused people to become distressed, suffering physical illnesses, psychological burnout, depression, low job satisfaction, the desire to change jobs, and even the inclination to behave dishonestly was less the workplace itself than how one's attitudes interacted with conditions within the workplace. Right away we knew we were on a journey that could not only impact the workforce but have far wider applications as well. This was an important finding because there are some jobs, working conditions, and even living environments that have an innately high potential to be distressing (air traffic control, law enforcement, international relief work, and warfare, for example).

While we may have little power to change the toxic potential of many such situations, the good news is that we don't necessarily have to change these environments to protect those who work and live within them. We learned that the attitudes and other psychological characteristics of the people within those environments might yield the answers about immunity and resilience we sought. This was the initial breakthrough in our search for psychological body armor. But our quest did not end there.

Our evolving work took us to the world of emergency services and disaster response. These services, many of which are performed by volunteers, include emergency medical services, law enforcement, search and rescue, body recovery, and fire suppression. Those who provide these services see, often on a daily basis, the side of society that most of us hope we will never experience. Some people have long and productive careers in emergency services; others do not. What distinguishes one group from the other?

The search further expanded and took us to a closer examination of Tom Brokaw's 1998 bestseller, *The Greatest Generation,* about the children of the Great Depression who experienced World War II. In Brokaw's words, "It is, I believe, the greatest generation any society has ever produced." They were united by duty, honor, courage, a strong sense of family and community, and a belief in self-responsibility. Were these to be the core factors that constituted our notion of psychological body armor? How does the greatest generation's value system compare with that of generation X and the millennials? And what does the answer to that question mean to the future of our country?

Finally, our interest turned to the military. The United States has found itself in one conflict after another. And as it did, suicides and posttraumatic stress disorder seemed to have reached epidemic proportions, but not for all. So we entered the world of elite special operations warriors in order to discover their "secret" of resilience. They run toward the sound of combat armed not only with extraordinary tactical skill but also with an unflappable optimism that they can and will succeed in whatever conflict they're called upon to address. Many of the conclusions and recommendations in this book emerged from studying the world of U.S. Navy SEALs. *SEAL* is an acronym reflecting the fact that these warriors are uniquely trained to conduct special warfare operations at sea, via the air, and on land.

The U.S. Navy SEALs are considered by many to be the most elite and effective military force the world has ever seen, and for good reason. Recently their extraordinary exploits have been the subjects of books and screenplays. The movie *Zero Dark Thirty* told the story of a SEAL team that was given speculative intelligence on the location of Osama Bin Laden. Armed with a unique optimism that it would find the world's most notorious terrorist, who had eluded capture for more than 10 years, SEAL Team SIX accepted the dangerous assignment to find Bin Laden. How much of the SEALs' success is a result of their unique skills, and how much is a result of their extraordinary optimism? Do they use that optimistic attitude as a competitive advantage—a resiliency advantage? Hold that thought.

How many instances do you know of athletes, businesspeople,

students, or performing artists who possessed extraordinary talent and even greater potential but never achieved the success for which they seemed destined? How many times have you heard that someone suffered from "performance anxiety," "burnout," or simply tended to "choke" under pressure? On the other hand, how often have you seen people rise from circumstances of adversity to do remarkable things, far exceeding anyone's expectations? How often have you heard of people excelling under pressure, rising up to meet a challenge, snatching "victory from the jaws of defeat"?

Such stories are legion, like that of a Scottish immigrant, Andrew Carnegie, who rose from laboring in a textile mill to dominating the world's steel-production industry; or Rosa Parks, who defied discrimination and demonstrated great courage when she refused to give up her seat on the bus, helping to spark a great change in America; or Nelson Mandela, James Stockdale, and John McCain, men of courage who enjoyed postimprisonment successes. The question is: Why do stress and pressure motivate individuals such as these to achieve success and personal growth, while they demotivate others and lead to disabling self-doubt and failure in critical situations? We believe those who can rise above adversity possess personal resilience. They even use it as a competitive advantage—a resiliency advantage.

In *Stronger*, we describe five core factors of personal resilience that:

1. Help people withstand adversity (a form of immunity)
2. Help people make good decisions under pressure
3. Motivate people to achieve peak performance
4. Allow people to bounce back quickly and effectively even when they are temporarily knocked down

5. Serve as important features in determining satisfaction in life and overall happiness

And the best news of all is that we believe these factors can be learned—at any age!

The opinions contained in this book were derived from original research, reviews of published research, personal experiences, clinical observations, and interviews conducted by the authors (formal and informal) with highly resilient people.

In this book, as we introduce you to the five factors of personal resilience, we will offer descriptions of and prescriptions for applying each of the five factors to your personal and professional lives. As noted, our descriptions and prescriptions are combinations of scientific analyses, scholarly and historical reviews, and the personal observations of the authors—three individuals (a clinician, a businessman, and a warrior) whose lives, while taking three very different paths, converged in an insatiable quest to understand remarkable success amid extraordinary adversity.

As we considered this project, we realized that in the ideal world, our five factors of personal resilience should be taught not only to our children but to anyone who aspires for immunity and resilience from stress, pressure, and adversity, conditions that seem almost epidemic in societies obsessed with performance and "success." Clearly, the ability to not only handle extreme stress and pressure but to excel in its midst can be life changing! It can be used as an advantage in almost any competitive situation, such as sports, academic placements, scholarships, entrepreneurship, auditions in the performing arts, or promotions in the workplace. And as we mentioned earlier, the foundations of personal resilience can be learned at any age. It's never too late. There are no magic bullets in this book. There are no miracle cures. But there are over 140 years of experience and collective insights that can change your life.

We end this preface with a simple theme adapted from an American adage: "Tomorrow is the first day of the rest of your life. And it is a gift." What are you going to do with this gift? Armed with personal resilience, almost anything becomes possible. But should you become hesitant as you ponder the options that life may reveal, just remember, "Anything worth having is worth failing for!" Now, it's up to you . . .

ACKNOWLEDGMENTS

I wish to thank all those who have shared with me over the last 40 years the stories of their journeys into the abyss and back. I'm especially appreciative to the "brotherhood of U.S. Navy SEALs," agents of the U.S. Federal Air Marshal Service and Bureau of Alcohol, Tobacco, Firearms and Explosives, and those individuals specifically profiled in this volume—heroes all. Gratitude is extended as well to Dr. Kenneth Smith for his friendship and research partnerships over the course of five decades. GSE

I would like to acknowledge my father-in-law, Dr. James Toher, who exemplified resilience. His dedication to his work, his family, and his patients served as an example for me of how to live one's life and serve others. DAS

To the Navy Frogmen of yesteryear, the Navy SEALs they have become today, and those who will join the ranks of SEALs in the future as members of an elite brotherhood of special operations warriors. Special thanks to my teammate Harry Monahan for his undying friendship over fifty-five years. Thanks to my doctoral classmates Barry Bultz and Sal Tagliareni for their ongoing support and friendship. DKM

———

Collective gratitude is extended to Captain Don Hinsvark, MA, Underwater Demolition Team Eleven, Naval Reserve Naval Special Warfare Detachment 119, U.S. Navy (retired) for his personal support and valuable contributions to this book. It never would have happened without Captain Hinsvark's support. Thanks also to Jacqueline Hinsvark for her help in concept formulation and refinement.

Thanks to Sarah Gieszl and Diane Gwin for their technical assistance.

Last, the authors wish to thank the folks at AMACOM who took our sometimes cryptic account of human resilience and turned it into a very practical guide on how to remain strong in the wake of adversity. Special thanks to:

Ellen Kadin, executive editor, who provided brilliant analyses presented in the form of compassionate guidance.

Erika B. Spelman, associate editor and copy manager, whose insightful perspectives strengthened the book in many different ways.

Louis Greenstein, developmental editor—as far as developmental editors go, he's the best of the best! Thank you Louis!

Ron Silverman, copyeditor, for his skillful editing and engaging queries.

Thanks to you all!

The authors are deeply indebted to the Navy SEAL Foundation. A portion of the authors' royalties will be donated to the Navy SEAL Foundation toward furthering the Foundation's valuable work.

CHAPTER 1

ACTIVE OPTIMISM AND THE SELF-FULFILLING PROPHECY

"In times of conflict or uncertainty there is a special person ready to answer the call; a common person, with an uncommon desire to succeed. I am that person. I stand ready to bring the full spectrum of resources to bear in order to achieve my goals. . . . In the worst of conditions . . . I will not fail." These words, adapted from the U.S. Navy SEAL Ethos, describe the type of person most of us would like to be. They certainly describe the type of person most businesses want to employ—and rapidly promote. But what do these people have that others don't?

What is the secret of experiencing extreme adversity and bouncing back stronger than you were before? More than 40 years ago, we set out to try to answer that question. Interestingly enough, setbacks, even failure, are a common experience associated with almost all human endeavors.

Everyone reading this book has faced adversity, and each has failed at least once in life. The issue is neither adversity nor failure per se, but what happens in the wake of adversity when you find yourself in the dark abyss of despair. Successful people fail. Happy people fail. The key doesn't lie in the nature of the adversity. What really matters is the degree of *personal resilience* you possess in the wake of the adversity.

PERSONAL RESILIENCE DEFINED

Personal resilience, what we sometimes think of as psychological body armor, is your ability to bounce back, to pick yourself up and try again, and again and again, until you either succeed or decide on a more productive direction. Resilience is your ability to see yourself in the dark abyss of failure, humiliation or depression—and bounce back, not only to where you were before, but to even greater heights of success, happiness, and inner strength. Resilience helps you withstand adversity. Think of it as a form of immunity that helps you make good decisions under pressure, motivates you for the achievement of peak performance, and allows you to bounce back quickly and effectively.

Science has shown that not only can you rebound from adversity and trauma, but you can also grow to be better than you ever were. As George Eliot once noted, "It is never too late to be what you might have been."

FIVE FACTORS OF PERSONAL RESILIENCE

From our research we concluded that successful people share a set of five core factors that equip them with personal resilience. Just as a suit of physical body armor protects the wearer from physical injury, it seems to us that a suit of psychological body armor can protect you against psychological distress and emotional injury. We believe that our five factors of personal resilience enable people, organizations, and even entire communities to withstand or rebound from adversity. They enable us to see opportunity in crisis. In psychologically toxic environments, they enable us to grow stronger.

Our goal for this book is to share with you the five factors of personal resilience and to show you ways you can develop this psychological body armor for yourself and foster it in others. While we have written about our preliminary findings on this topic in scientific and more readily accessible formats, this book represents our sometimes startling new conclusions, honed through more than four decades of research and experiential refinement.

Our five factors of personal resilience are:

1. *Active Optimism*. Optimism is more than a belief, it's a mandate for change. It's the inclination to move forward when others are retreating. This mandate can be so strong that it can become a self-fulfilling prophecy. But to do so it must lead to . . .

2. *Decisive Action*. Optimism is not enough. You must be decisive and act in order to rebound. As Clare Boothe Luce observed, "Courage is the ladder on which all the other virtues mount." You must acquire the courage to make difficult decisions. Making hard decisions is easier when it is based upon a . . .

3. *Moral Compass*. Use honor, integrity, fidelity, and ethical behavior to guide your decisions under challenging circumstances. Once your decisions have been implemented, employ . . .

4. *Relentless Tenacity, Determination.* Persistence can be omnipotent. As comedian Jonathan Winters once quipped, "If
your ship doesn't come, swim out to meet it!" Be persistent,
while at the same time knowing when to quit. To find hidden opportunities and aid in physical and psychological energy, rely upon . . .

5. *Interpersonal Support.* Who has your back?

BIOLOGICAL BASES OF HUMAN RESILIENCE

In order to appreciate the power of human resilience it might be
helpful to understand its foundations. It may surprise you to learn
that resilience as we have just defined it has biological foundations
as well as psychological ones. So let's take a quick look at the biology of resilience.

In 1975, neurologist Paul MacLean coined the term *triune brain*
to describe its three functional levels: The neocortex is the most
sophisticated component of the human brain, representing its
highest functioning level. Not only does the neocortex interpret
sensory signals, communications, and gross proprioceptive-based
control of motor (musculoskeletal) behaviors, but part of it—the
ventromedial prefrontal cortex (vmPFC)—presides over imagination, logic, decision making, problem solving, planning, apprehension, and, most important, the interpretation of experience. It is the
vmPFC that labels an experience (real or imagined) as threatening,
punishing, or rewarding. It finds solutions to problems, it sees the
opportunity in danger, and it sees the glass as half full rather than
half empty. Based on the nature of the interpretation of experience,
the vmPFC then activates the second level of the triune brain: the
limbic system.

The limbic system is relevant in any discussion of stress and resilience because of its role as the human brain's emotional control center. The limbic system is believed to be just that, a system, consisting of numerous highly connected neural structures, for example, the hypothalamus, hippocampus, septum, cingulate gyrus, and the amygdala. The amygdala is the primary anatomic center for fear, anger, trauma, and aggression. It's also the center of the *fight-or-flight response*, a term coined by psychologist Walter Cannon in 1915. The amygdala serves as the primary survival mechanism in the human body. Thus, it's a key anatomic component in the biology of resilience.

The brain stem and spinal cord represent the lowest level of the triune brain. The major functions of this level are the maintenance of so-called vegetative roles such as heartbeat, respiration, vasomotor activity, and the conduction of impulses to many higher levels of the brain. The spinal cord represents the central pathway for neurons as they conduct signals to and from the brain. The brain stem is the basic engine that drives the machinery of the human body.

Human resilience represents a most elegant and ongoing dance between the vmPFC and the amygdala. When faced with danger, the vmPFC activates the amygdala so as to prepare you to fight, flee, or otherwise resolve the threat. Highly resilient people appear to be able to effectively regulate the amygdala so as to benefit from its activation but then allow it to quickly recover its baseline activity. This process of recovery to a steady state is what Cannon called "the reestablishment of homeostasis."

Consequently, the bodies of resilient people are supercharged with moderate increases in hormones such as adrenalin, noradrenalin, gamma-Aminobutyric acid, neuropeptide Y and cortisol, which allow you to do "superhuman" things for short periods of time. When these hormones surge, your strength and perception increase, your memory improves, your eyesight may get better, your tolerance for pain increases, and you react to stimuli faster. In other words, you're better prepared to meet any challenge successfully.

The person who is not resilient experiences homeostatic failure, during which the vmPFC interpretations either overstimulate or understimulate the limbic system. The result of overstimulation can be anxiety, panic attacks, confusion, reduced problem-solving capacity, irritability, anger, even violence (for example, road rage, airline rage), and seizures. The result of understimulation may be hopelessness, depression, resentment, and a lack of motivation. With highly frequent or chronic overstimulation the amygdala can develop a state of chronic hypersensitivity at the cellular level. Amygdaloid nerve cells literally become highly irritable and will overrespond to experiences that would have not otherwise caused excitation. It's like having 10 cups of coffee.

So the key to developing resilience at the biological level is to train your brain to regulate its downstream physiology and to interpret experience in such a manner that activation occurs so as to increase performance, but also allows for rapid homeostasis. Research has shown that neuropeptide Y, a neurotransmitter, can be enhanced by resilience training. Changing psychological attitudes is the key. The most powerful attitude of all may be optimism.

SELF-ASSESSMENTS

Sun Tzu, the great Chinese military strategist, wrote, "He who knows the enemy and himself will never in a hundred battles be at risk." So let's start by getting to know you a little better. In each chapter of this book, we have included a simple resilience self-assessment so you can assess just how many elements of personal resilience (psychological body armor) you already have. These self-assessments can serve several purposes:

- They will give you a quick snapshot of the current status of each of our five factors of resilience.
- They can serve as a resilience monitor that can help you assess the impact of stressful life events that might occur.
- They will help you see what impact your efforts have had in increasing your personal resilience as you begin to implement the prescriptions in this book.

SELF-ASSESSMENT #1

Directions: Circle the answer that best describes how strongly you agree with the following statements.

1. *I am truly thankful for the positive things in life.*
   1—Strongly disagree
   2—Disagree
   3—Agree
   4—Strongly agree

2. *I hope that my life will be happy and rewarding.*
   1—Strongly disagree
   2—Disagree
   3—Agree
   4—Strongly agree

3. I expect life to be positive and rewarding.

    1—Strongly disagree

    2—Disagree

    3—Agree

    4—Strongly agree

4. I do not wait for good things to happen, I make them happen.

    1—Strongly disagree

    2—Disagree

    3—Agree

    4—Strongly agree

5. When I encounter challenges and even failures, I know I will be successful in time.

    1—Strongly disagree

    2—Disagree

    3—Agree

    4—Strongly agree

This self-assessment is not a clinical diagnostic tool. It is simply a survey designed to motivate you to think about your attitudes concerning optimism. When you've completed the survey, add up the numbers next to the answers you have circled. The lowest possible score is 5, and the highest is 20. The higher your score, the more actively optimistic you are likely to be. There will be more on this later in the chapter. For now, though, let's take a closer look at the quality of optimism and how it affects human resilience.

ACTIVE OPTIMISM

Perpetual optimism, believing in yourself, believing in your purpose, believing you will prevail, and demonstrating passion and confidence is a force multiplier.

— COLIN POWELL

So, as we mentioned earlier, there are five personal factors that, when combined, serve as a force multiplier, increasing your capacity to be more effective than you would be otherwise. These characteristics provide the unique advantage of resiliency to those who possess them. The first such characteristic is active optimism.

Optimism is the tendency to take the most positive or hopeful view of matters. It's the tendency to expect the best outcome; the belief that good will prevail over evil.

But the value of optimism is much greater than just the good mood that can accompany a rosy outlook. In fact, research tells us that optimists possess qualities that are much more likely to make them not only happier but more successful than their pessimistic brothers and sisters.

The optimist always has the capacity to look forward to another day. Not surprising then that optimistic people are more likely to persevere. They are not only more resilient than pessimists but better able to tolerate adversity, more task oriented, and committed to success. And, again, perhaps not surprising, optimists tend to experience depression less than pessimists.

When you ask people whether they're optimists, most will say yes. The few who don't will generally prefer to call themselves realists rather than pessimists. With that in mind, we tried to separate the real optimists from the wannabes through formal and informal interviews with a group of people who included a number of Navy SEALs. We asked not only whether they were optimists but also about the specific characteristics that made them that way. Their answers were revealing because an interesting dichotomy began to emerge: There are actually two types of optimism—passive and active.

Passive optimists *hope* things will turn out well and *believe* that they will. But those who merely hope and believe are surrendering control of their circumstances to someone, or something else. Active optimists, on the other hand, *act* in a way that increases the likelihood that things will indeed turn out well. Many of the SEALs we have known described this kind of optimism as a "mandate" to create a positive future.

So let's take a closer look at the epitome of active optimism. As we mentioned earlier, Navy SEALs seem to share the characteristic of a strong positive mental attitude—an expectation of personal success. For SEALs, the difference between success and failure is often the difference between life and death. From the SEAL perspective, success doesn't just happen by chance; it happens because you *make* it happen. The optimistic expectation of success occurs because of relentless preparation, understanding only too well the meaning of sacrifice, coupled with dogged determination. The SEALs' success begins with active optimism—a positive attitude and a mandate to change the world.

Of course, not all active optimists think in such emphatic terms; but all active optimists do believe they can make a difference. They choose to take control over their circumstances, and often their lives. They are never out of the fight. Active optimists move *toward* the sound of distress and despair because they believe they can change things for the better. They see opportunities in adversity, which makes them good problem solvers. Active optimists such as "Moki" Martin expect, and often create, success.

PHILIP L. "MOKI" MARTIN, U.S. NAVY SEAL

Philip L. "Moki" Martin was born in Hawaii on September 16, 1942. He grew up in and around water. Swimming and diving in the ocean were as natural to him as breathing. Martin enjoyed meeting the many challenges that ocean swimming brought and discovered that the more difficult the tasks he encountered, the more he automatically began to program himself to think only in terms of success.

The ocean, with its unpredictable currents and waves, helped Martin develop an attitude of active optimism, the belief that no matter what unforeseen challenge the ocean might present, he would be able to survive. This is what some refer to as self-efficacy. The word *failure*—which, in the ocean, meant certain death—was not in his vocabulary. This powerful attitude produced a resiliency advantage throughout Martin's life.

As the United States entered the conflict in Southeast Asia, Martin fulfilled his dream of becoming a Navy Frogman and SEAL, successfully coping with the rigors of what many considered the toughest military training program in the world. Martin was sent to Vietnam to face the greatest challenge of his life in the service of his country.

Because Martin's story was classified for 35 years, it has only recently been told. In 1972, he was a member of U.S. Navy SEAL Team ONE, Alpha Platoon, based on Okinawa. June of that year saw Alpha Platoon ordered to take part in the top secret Operation Thunderhead.

The first part of the mission entailed having the SEALs rendezvous with the USS *Grayback* in Subic Bay, Philippines. The *Grayback* was a submarine converted to support clandestine special operations involving SEALs as well as underwater demolition teams using special-delivery vehicles (SDVs). SDVs, sometimes affectionately referred to as mini-submarines, would normally have a pilot and navigator, and space for two SEAL passengers.

Subsequent to the rendezvous, the mission entailed having a *Grayback*-housed SDV deliver the SEALs to an island off the coast of North Vietnam. The SEALs were to look for two U.S. prisoners of war who would be making their way down the Red River to the Gulf of Tonkin after escaping from captivity.

The two POWs were pilots who were being held prisoner in a camp near Hanoi, North Vietnam. The pilots were to escape during a planned diversionary air raid on Hanoi, make their way to the Red River, find a boat by whatever means, and make their way downstream to the Gulf of Tonkin for pickup by a rescue helicopter.

On June 3, 1972, in preparation for the planned escape, Lieutenant Melvin Spence Dry's SEAL team, including Warrant Officer Moki Martin, attempted to conduct a clandestine reconnaissance in North Vietnamese-controlled territory, not far from Hinan Island, which was Chinese controlled. After the team deployed from the *Grayback*, strong ocean currents prevented it from achieving its objective.

The SEALs were picked up from the open ocean and taken to the USS *Long Beach* with the intention of reuniting with the *Grayback* via helicopter two days later. This would require a night water drop next to the submarine. During briefings with the helicopter pilots, Lt. Dry and Martin emphasized that the maximum limits for the drop were 20/20 (20 feet of altitude at an airspeed of 20 knots) or an equivalent combination.

Because of rough seas, the rendezvous with the *Grayback* was canceled, but word did not reach the helicopter carrying the SEALs. The pilot signaled the SEALs to jump from what he thought was a height of 20 feet and speed of 20 knots. However, the height of the helicopter exceeded 50 feet, and a significant tailwind was pushing it at unacceptable speeds. Lt. Dry died upon impact due to severe neck trauma, according to the navy's death report. Another team member was seriously injured upon impact and rendered unconscious. Martin was injured but survived the jump and began searching for his teammates. He reached the unconscious team member and inflated his life vest, saving him.

Martin and his team later found Dry's body. They inflated his life vest and held him in tow as they swam seaward to be rescued.

The loss of his friend and teammate weighed heavily on Martin, but he knew he was responsible for the rest of the team. He maintained a vigilant watch over them throughout the night, as a rough sea and high winds prevented a rescue. "I will never leave a teammate behind," Martin told us.

With enemy boats patrolling the area, Martin had the responsibility of leading his team to safety. Radio contact with the rescue helicopters onboard the USS *Long Beach* was challenging because the North Vietnamese were monitoring their radio frequencies. Nevertheless, Martin established contact, but only after he and his team spent a long, cold night in the ocean.

An HC-7 helicopter rescued the men at dawn and returned them to the *Long Beach*. Because the mission was classified, the navy did not acknowledge Dry's death as a combat loss until February 2008, when he was posthumously awarded the Bronze Star for valor. He was the last U.S. Navy SEAL to die in the Vietnam War.

Martin exuded confidence and optimism his whole life. This philosophy created an atmosphere among his team members that led them to take on the challenges of a very long swim to safety in enemy-controlled waters. Martin's optimism and selfless leadership was a major factor in their safe return to the USS *Grayback*.

Upon his return to the United States, Martin was made a SEAL instructor in 1976 and stationed at Coronado Island across the bay from San Diego, California. He was able to return to his normal routines, one of which was maintaining physical conditioning. In fact, Martin was one of the early proponents of today's organized triathlons.

Then, on a foggy morning in October 1982, while on a training bicycle ride down the seven mile strand beach on Highway 75, connecting Coronado Island to Imperial Beach, Martin ran head-on into a bicyclist coming from the opposite direction. The cyclists crashed with such impact that Martin sustained a spinal cord injury that left him a quadriplegic, confined to a wheelchair for the rest of his life.

To keep disaster from turning into ruin, Martin enlisted the power of active optimism. He harnessed the same positive mental attitude that allowed him to become a world-class swimmer in Hawaii, to be a member of the elite brotherhood of Navy SEALs, to serve with valor during war, and subsequently to be a supportive husband and father.

Martin knew that he would get back on course and that his life was going to continue. The navy retired Martin, but to a status known (appropriately) as active retired.

He returned to college, completing his bachelor's degree with a major in applied arts and science. He became a painter. One of his professors at San Diego State University, the artist Janet Cooling, said, "Moki has always touched me with his honesty, continuing openness to life, and art, and an eagerness to grapple with ideas, . . . Moki is a profound artist." As one door closes, another door opens to those who believe in themselves and continually see the opportunities in adversity.

Martin benefited from the support of others, but he never relinquished the desire to provide support and leadership, and to serve as a role model for others who encounter adversity.

Martin continues to be involved with his community and is on-call 24/7 to help those in need. For the past 35 years he has spearheaded fundraising efforts for military veterans and families through his Super SEAL Triathlon and Super SEAL Marathon in Coronado, California. He also manages to find the time to return to his SEAL training roots: He lectures on "Lessons Learned in Viet Nam" at the Naval Special Warfare Center in Coronado, has been race director for the Naval Special Warfare "Superfrog" triathlon competition, and is involved with Superfrog Triathlons Inc.

On March 18, 2008, Martin was awarded the navy and Marine Corps Commendation Medal with a combat V for valor. He was cited for valor for his part in the rescue of his two injured SEAL team members, and for preserving the body of Lt. Dry until recovery. At that ceremony, Martin said, "I accept this award on behalf of all of you from Alpha Platoon. This award is for all of you."

Fast forward; the man standing before a group of military trainees is a Navy SEAL. His job is to teach the trainees how to prevail in a knife fight. He stares coldly into the eyes of his students. He knows that in order to win a knife fight, one must possess not only the skill but also the belief. And he knows that the fear of being injured must be confronted directly. He says simply, but forcefully:

"What I will teach you will cause you to be the victor in a struggle for life and death. You will get cut. You will bleed. But never lose sight of the fact that you will survive that fight. Your adversary will not!"

In this situation, the instructor is telling his students that they will be successful, but success comes with a cost. He knows there is a high probability that his student will be injured, and he also knows that the fear of the injury may be more debilitating than the injury itself. Thus, getting cut should be seen as merely a temporary setback on the road to success and victory.

This story can serve as a metaphor that's applicable to all aspects of life when you face adversity and encounter setbacks. Sometimes, adversity may seem potentially devastating. The key is in how you interpret the setback. Green Bay Packers football coach Vince Lombardi once said, "We didn't lose the game. We simply ran out of time."

RESILIENCE AND THE GIFT OF FAILURE

It may seem odd to describe failure as a gift. But highly successful and resilient people know that it can be.

Al Neuharth, founder of the USA Today publishing empire; Cal Ripken Jr., one of the greatest baseball players of all time; Michael Jordan, voted the greatest athlete of the 20th century by ESPN; and even Thomas Edison, the greatest inventor of the 20th century, all agree that failure was a necessary aspect of their subsequent success.

Neuharth's first newspaper went bankrupt, and *USA Today* lost millions of dollars before not only succeeding but revolutionizing print journalism. Neuharth went on to found the Freedom Forum and the Newseum. He wrote in his 1989 autobiography that failure shouldn't stop your drive to succeed. Rather, it's how you respond to failure that makes all the difference.

For baseball's Cal Ripken, success is celebrated, because "we . . . find out who we are in failure." The reflections on failure of basketball's Michael Jordan were a hit Nike commercial and today adorn posters from corporate boardrooms to kids' bedrooms:

"I've missed more than 9000 shots in my career. I've lost almost 300 games. 26 times, I've been trusted to take the game
winning shot and missed. I've failed over and over and over
again in my life. And that is why I succeed."

Think of a rubber ball. In order to make it bounce back you
must put it under great pressure. The greater the pressure, the
higher the ball will bounce back. Now to be clear, it's not the pressure itself that causes the ball to bounce, but the construction and
attributes of the ball under pressure. It's what the ball is made of
that really matters. The pressure serves as a catalyst for the rebound.

Take the example of strength training. Lifting weights will
make you stronger and will increase the size of your muscles.
How? The stress of lifting creates tears in microscopic muscle fi-
bers. The body then uses internal nutrients, especially protein and
anabolic hormones, to repair this damage. If these reparative attributes are available in sufficient amounts, the muscle will actually increase in size and strength. You can grow your muscles by
lifting light or heavy weights. It's not the weight per se that causes
the muscles to grow but the internal physiological attributes and
nutritional resources interacting with the catalyst of weightlifting.

A grizzled Olympic weightlifting coach once remarked, "No
one ever left the gym stronger than they entered. If you train right
your workout always leaves you weaker, but you will wake up the
next day stronger than you were the day before." Sometimes in
order to get stronger, you must first get weaker.

It should be mentioned that extraordinary pressure has been
known to damage the ball. Similarly, if you lift weights but neglect

to rest long enough for your muscles to heal, you can damage your-self. But for the most part, stress, adversity, and even failure can lead to greater strength and greater success. They can make you stronger.

THE MOST TOXIC THOUGHTS YOU CAN HAVE

In 1989, we collaborated with Professor Kenneth Smith in an effort to identify workplace predictors of burnout. Burnout may be thought of as a state of physical, mental, and emotional exhaustion, often subsequently related to accidents, divorce, overall poor quality of life on the job and at home, and even dishonesty in the workplace.

With Professor Smith, we investigated low job satisfaction, poor job performance, and the intention to quit one's job (a costly expense to employers, especially if the individual holds a key position). Over the next 20 years, we used statistical modeling techniques to create a virtual reality of human health and disease—and a very consistent, remarkable finding emerged.

We discovered that a psychological pattern of repetitive worry and negativity was a better predictor of burnout, low job satisfaction, poor job performance, and the intention to quit one's job than were actual environmental/situational workplace factors, such as conflicts on the job, ambiguous work instructions and environments, and burdensome job demands. Further, to our surprise, this toxic psychological attitude seemed to predict physical illness as long as one year later. Our findings echo the words of the character Chareos in David Gemmell's fantasy novel *Quest for Lost Heroes*:

"Do not speak badly of yourself, for the warrior that is inside you hears your words and is lessened by them. You are strong and you are brave. There is a nobility of spirit within you. Let it grow—you will do well enough."

Our findings also suggest that a person's attitude on the job, and possibly in life in general, are as important as or more important than the working or living environment itself. Attitudes can be toxic or they can be protective. These findings are certainly consistent with the Greek philosopher Epictetus's famous observation, "Men are disturbed, not by things, but the views which they take of them." Similarly, we are reminded of Milton's classic *Paradise Lost:* "The mind is its own place and in itself, can make a Heaven of Hell, a Hell of Heaven."

Some jobs by their very nature are stressful and dangerous, yet someone must do them. Sometimes, through no fault of your own, life becomes challenging or even traumatic. How can you withstand the pain of adversity? How do you rise above life's calamities? Our research suggests that your attitude is critical. And the good news is that attitudes can be taught—and changed.

危机—CRISIS AND ACTIVE OPTIMISM

When written in Chinese, the word *crisis* is expressed with two characters: 危机. Those characters may be interpreted as "danger" and "possibility." It has been suggested, therefore, that a crisis represents a dangerous opportunity—but only to those who possess the vision to see it. That's active optimism.

It's during times of crisis that the true nature of active optimism is revealed. Active optimists are able to recognize the potential for hidden opportunities within a crisis and take advantage of them. Such vision provides opportunities for great competitive advantage. But when there's no value to be gained from the crisis, the optimist is able to conserve resources (cut losses) and patiently wait for another opportunity. The ability to delay gratification, control what you can, and cope with what you can't is essential.

Being an entrepreneur is a risky business. According to the U.S. Bureau of Labor Statistics, 49 percent of businesses survive five years or more; 34 percent survive 10 years or more; and only 26 percent survive 15 years or more.

Entrepreneurs are risk takers by anyone's standard. OK, so you may be wondering, why do risk takers take risks? That's easy. They don't see what they're doing as risky. That's active optimism at work. Entrepreneurs such as Andrew Carnegie do tend to be active optimists.

The years 1869 to 1873 were economically challenging for the United States. September 24, 1869, saw speculation and manipulations in the U.S. gold markets that resulted in an ounce of gold climbing to a price of almost $163 from $143—and then rapidly declining. Wall Street brokerage houses collapsed as investors lost fortunes. Railroad stocks crumbled, and the nation's economy felt like chaos as credit was frozen. Leading financial institutions were thrust into bankruptcy. Businesses were paralyzed.

Then the year 1871 saw the Great Chicago Fire, while 1872 saw an equine epidemic of influenza that left America without a viable means of local transportation. It even left the storied U.S. Cavalry horseless.

The post–Civil War era of overproduction and deflation, fueled by economic hardships in Europe, reached a crescendo when another financial collapse occurred on Friday, September 19, 1873. The New York Stock Exchange closed for 10 days as railroad construction stopped and railroads defaulted on loans. This era of adversity drove the price of steel to less than a penny a pound.

This certainly seemed like no time to invest in the steel industry. But that's exactly what Andrew Carnegie did. Between 1870 and 1872, he built two blast furnaces. Envisioning an economic rebirth and prosperity, over the next two years he mass-produced inexpensive steel for industry, including the railroads. Guided by an unflappable optimism, Carnegie boldly and persistently expanded his steel business into a vertically integrated empire until his business became the world's largest steel company and he the world's wealthiest man. Ironically, much of the current federal antitrust legislation came about because of the previously unheard of success of people like Carnegie.

As we've mentioned, rather than retreat in the face of adversity, active optimists move toward the sound of distress and despair, because they believe they can change things for the better. At one time or another, each of us faces adversity, but co-author Douglas Strouse and his family faced a challenge unlike most.

DOUGLAS A. STROUSE, PH.D.

Suicide is a silent epidemic that claims a life every 18 minutes. More than 30,000 Americans die of suicide every year. It's the third-leading cause of death for ages 15 to 24 in the United States.

Though she had been having a hard time adjusting to college as a freshman, I could never conceive of anyone committing suicide—much less *my* daughter.

Approximately 10 days had passed since the time we got the phone call saying she had died to the time we buried my little girl. During that time I know I barely slept and ate very little. I was not going to the gym (my usual stress-management tool) and of course did not go into the office. I made a strong effort to resume my life as well as possible, to get up early, work out and go to work, even though my daughter was on my mind throughout each and every day. I was constantly seeing things that made me think of her, and tears would usually come to my eyes. People, just in the course of conversation, would sometimes remark, "I would just kill myself" if such and such happened, and that comment would take me back to my daughter's death in an instant. It was a constant struggle to regain my footing back in the "real world." I knew that the death of a child was a burden that could potentially cripple me. I also knew that many marriages that suffered the death of a child ended in divorce.

After a couple of months had passed, my family decided that we would not be passive. We needed to do something to help ourselves and to help others. I was not going to be a victim. I was not going to let our marriage be a victim. If we could save just one child's life!

Although we knew nothing about the illness that took my daughter's life, and although we knew nothing about charitable foundations, we decided to move forward rather than retreat in the face of a pain no parent should ever have to experience. We decided we would create a nonprofit foundation in my little girl's name whose mission would be to raise awareness about and reduce the stigma associated with mental health issues, and promote the prevention of teenage suicide—and maybe it could save marriages as well.

Today the Kristin Rita Strouse Foundation has donated over $1.5 million in support to the Johns Hopkins department of psychiatry; the Rita Project's studios in New York City, Baltimore, and Los Angeles, which use the arts to help those who have survived a suicide attempt as well as those who have lived through the suicide of a loved one connect with the power of creativity; the American Foundation for Suicide Prevention's (AFSP) College Film Project; the AFSP's College Screening Project; the AFSP's Out of the Darkness Walks; and the Depression and Related Affective Disorders Association, among other organizations and activities.

As I look back now over a decade, I learned life does go on. It will never be the same, but it does go on. You have to go on; it's too easy to give in. You have to grow. I also learned I'm an optimist who must make a difference. It's who I am and what I've always done.

ACTIVE OPTIMISM AND THE SELF-FULFILLING PROPHECY

The ultimate function of prophecy is not to tell the future, but to make it.
—W. WARREN WAGAR, *Prophecies of a World Civilization*
in Twentieth-Century Thought

The most powerful source of active optimism appears to be the experience of success itself. Success begets success. The more successes you have, the better you'll understand what it takes to be successful—which will generate more successes—and the more you will tend to expect success. This also sets the stage for the emergence of self-fulfilling prophecy, which promotes active optimism even further. So let's take a closer look at this remarkable phenomenon.

Victory always starts with a state of mind. It then spreads with such radiance that destiny can do nothing but obey. The self-fulfilling prophecy can be a tremendous competitive advantage. It is the embodiment of the notion that any prediction about a human behavior actually affects the behavior itself. Your state of mind really matters! If you believe that you will succeed, your chance of success increases. On the other hand, if you believe that you will fail, your chance of failure increases.

This is consistent with the research we conducted with Kenneth Smith. If you recall, we discovered that worry and negative thoughts seemed to predict job-related problems and even physical illness. Why is this so? It's not magic. If you think you will fail at something, you are likely to attempt the task with minimal effort, enthusiasm, and tenacity. You are more willing to accept initial rejection or failure. In addition, you are more likely to view the world as a stressful place. The more stress you experience in your life, the greater your chances of becoming physically ill. Research has shown, for example, that stress reduces your immune system's ability to defend against bacteria, viruses, and even cancer.

On the other hand, if you think you will succeed at something, you are likely to attempt the task with greater effort, enthusiasm, and tenacity. You are less willing to accept initial rejection or failure. You are more likely to see those occurrences as exceptions to the rule and simply precursors of your inevitable success. You are more likely to be physically healthier. And, as the following story illustrates, you will find that your positive beliefs affect your performance.

Two friends were playing golf. They stood on an elevated tee box overlooking a 160-yard par three hole. In between the tee and the green was a pond.

The first golfer reached into his bag to find an older golf ball. The second golfer asked what he was doing.

"I'm using an old ball in case I hit into the water," the first golfer said. He then hit the ball—that's right—into the water. The second golfer hit his ball safely onto the green.

As they were moving to the green, the second golfer said, "You know why you hit into the water don't you?"

"Yes," the first golfer replied. "I hit a bad shot."

"No," the second golfer responded, "You hit into the water because you prepared to hit into the water. You expected to hit into the water. When I teed my ball, I didn't even notice the pond. All I saw was green."

A belief can affect your body's physiology beyond your immune system. In a fascinating study conducted decades ago, patients diagnosed with panic disorder were randomly assigned to one of two groups. Both groups were asked to breathe air that had been infused with carbon dioxide (CO_2) sufficient to cause a panic attack. Group A was given access to a dial that, when turned, they were told, would reduce the CO_2 and thus reduce the chance of a panic attack. Group B was not given that access.

As expected, only 20 percent of the patients in Group A experienced a panic attack, while 80 percent of Group B experienced panic. But interestingly, the dial that Group A turned did not actually work. That group thought it was no longer breathing CO_2, when in fact it was breathing the same amount of CO_2 as Group B. Thus, the panic was prevented by the belief/expectation, not the dial. The ability to resist panic was a self-fulfilling prophecy.

Sadly, the fact is that many people consistently turn the power of the self-fulfilling prophecy against themselves. They are taught and encouraged to prepare for failure.

As children, many of us were told, "Now don't get your hopes up." Or, "Just try your best, but don't be disappointed. After all, there can only be one winner." Parents can sabotage their children's success by teaching them it's OK to aspire to mediocrity, or to accept failure as a likely outcome of their efforts. The intentions are well meaning; these parents aim to protect their children against the pain of disappointment, while hoping that they will gradually become proficient. The problem is that those early messages often create a toxic expectation of mediocrity or failure. In some cases, children are neglected or abused into a lifelong spiral of negativity and self-defeating behavior with little opportunity to bounce back. Not so for Abbey-Robin Tillery.

ABBEY-ROBIN TILLERY, PH.D.

Clinical psychologist Abbey-Robin Tillery's story is one of self-fulfilling prophecy. She graduated from the International Baccalaureate Program, received a commission as a captain in the U.S Army, and completed her Ph.D. all before age 26. Her contributions to the field of military psychology, resilience, and early intervention have resulted in the formation of numerous clinics and working groups, national support programs, and innovations in delivery of psychological support around the world.

Today at age 34, as a Department of Defense psychologist, she occupies a position of trust and responsibility within the U.S. government and has brought innovations to defense intelligence and U.S. embassy security throughout the world. However, statistically, Tillery should not have accomplished any of this.

Tillery never had a supportive childhood or a stable, loving home. Her childhood was riddled with chronic sexual abuse, parental neglect, poverty, and psychological chaos. In an incredible leap of faith, she made the courageous decision to emancipate herself at age 15. In secrecy from her peers and teachers, she ended up changing residences multiple times before graduating from high school.

Without parental support, Tillery was unable to attend the private university that had accepted her. However, she again saw opportunities around the corner and attended an excellent state school, the University of Colorado. Once enrolled, she began to thrive against the odds, creating multiple groups, projects, and networks that caught the attention of the top professors, all without having a solid place to call home.

She earned her BA in three years and was accepted into a Ph.D. program affiliated with Stanford University. After only a year in graduate school, she began the entrepreneurial approach that characterized her academic life and cofounded an early intervention clinic for acute stress disorder. This was a joint venture she initiated between the Menlo Park and Palo Alto VA hospitals, Stanford University, and Palo Alto University.

Professional success does not always translate into personal maturity, however, and Tillery fell prey to a deeply abusive, exploitive relationship, despite being "so smart." This was the beginning of the darkest times in her life.

While she was making great strides academically in college, she was leading a double life; one side of her was setting records and winning awards while the other side was being manipulated and controlled. She was coerced into turning over the money from all of her signature loans and had to work three part-time jobs while in graduate school just to survive. The San Francisco Bay Area turned out to be more expensive than even three part-time jobs could sustain, and she faced homelessness after only a year into her Ph.D. program.

Rather than quit and return to a chaotic life she knew would destroy her, Tillery pursued what she believed to be her destiny. She found a way to finance a sailboat and live aboard it, albeit with questionable legality, while she completed her schooling. She had no running water on board, no way to cook, no bathroom; she ate food out of teachers' and student lounges, doctors' lounges, and sometimes helped herself—without paying—at Sunday brunches at surrounding hotels. Tillery was able to sustain this fragile existence for two years.

An average day involved attending a lecture at Stanford and then finding herself without enough money to drive back to the boat, necessitating spending the night on the floor in the lab where she worked. Some days she would wake up to fog in her boat because she had to choose between powering her computer and powering a space heater; other days she would have to pump water out of the boat because the bilge pump failed, all while keeping the commitments she had made to so many important projects and people.

An unplanned pregnancy occurred in her fourth year of school, a result of the ongoing abusive relationship. She wondered if this would finally topple her house of cards.

The pregnancy coincided with her dissertation year, and she found ways to make this work. She gave birth at Stanford Hospital but had to take the baby back to the boat and contend with a deeply dysfunctional secret life.

The darkest point in her life turned out to also be what saved her. In 2006, she was confronted with irrefutable evidence that the person who had been so controlling and abusive was also a fraud. Tillery wanted to quit life. She felt she could not call herself a psychologist after being so deeply deceived, nor did she feel she could wear the army uniform. Who would respect her?

After two horrible years of self-doubt, agonizingly twisting in the wind (yes, even optimists have self-doubt at times), she finally gained the courage to tell others what she had endured and how she stumbled. Thankfully, their response was compassionate. They helped her fully reconnect to herself, her dream, and her basic belief about herself.

An important turning point in Tillery's life was connecting with teachers who saw her as gifted and believed in her. These exceptional people provided just enough of a buffer between her tempestuous home and her intellectual gifts; their empathy helped her escape mentally before she could physically. Sometimes support comes in the form of a community.

Getting accepted into the community of the U.S. Army internship program was, for Tillery, the beginning of the relief from her abuser. Becoming an officer enabled her to move on with her life in a radically different way. For the first time ever, she had financial security, a tangible career, and a promising future. Because of the physical security and human resources the army provided her, she was able to emancipate herself for the second time from an abusive home life and lay the foundation for the rest of her livelihood. The army inadvertently was her halfway house, giving her just enough strength to be fully independent and provide for her child.

We are struck by the courage and determination of a young woman who didn't always know where she was going but knew that wherever it might be, it had to be better than where she was. Active optimistic imagination during the darkest points of Tillery's life provided hope; it ultimately helped her escape from the abyss, and it has enabled her to grow. Tillery always had a feeling she was special—a feeling that was totally unexplained and irrational from every perspective. This seeming delusion turned out to be one of the things that saved her.

"Finding a way to imagine a better life for oneself is the first step in making it happen," she told us. "Believe in yourself. Believe you are destined for something better. The belief will carry you far." She summarized her journey by saying, "There is a strong intuitive sense in us all that screams out against all odds, 'I will make it.'"

Probably the most critical use of self-fulfilling prophecy often occurs in the military, where it can directly influence a struggle for life itself. For example, U.S. Army General Hal Moore, who commanded during and after the Vietnam War, was selected as one of the greatest 100 generals to have ever lived. In his book *A Tender Warrior*, General Moore related telling a new group of soldiers under his command:

We're a good Battalion, but we're gonna get a hell of a lot better. I will do my best and expect the same from each of you. We
will be . . . without equal. We will be the best infantry Battalion
in the world! Now go back to your barracks and get rid of all
the 2nd place trophies. From now on, only 1st place trophies
will be awarded, accepted or displayed in this outfit. In our line
of work if we come in second, we are defeated on the battlefield. From now on, we are interested only in winning! We are
without equal!

RX: PRESCRIPTIONS FOR BUILDING ACTIVE OPTIMISM

Having described our notion of active optimism, we will now give
you specific methods, or prescriptions, for achieving active optimism.

Active optimism is similar to the construct of self-efficacy developed by psychologist Albert Bandura at Stanford University. In
Self-Efficacy: The Exercise of Control, his 1997 magnum opus on
human agency, Bandura argues that the optimistic belief in one's
ability to organize and execute the actions required to achieve necessary and desired goals can be taught using four modes of learning. Generally speaking, they are:

- *Personal Attainment*. Doing something, anything, successfully really matters. It reverses the pattern and the pain of
  failure. Current success predicts future success and will create active optimism. Allow yourself to have success, even if
  it's a small success at first. Small successes will become big
  successes with time, especially as your confidence grows.

- *Observation*. Another way to increase your sense of active optimism in to watch others be successful at things you desire to be successful at. This can serve to motivate you, especially if those you observe are somehow like you. "If they can do it, why can't I?"

- *Encouragement and Support*. If you're lucky enough to have supportive friends, family, and professional leaders (advisers, mentors), their encouragement will enhance your active optimism. Accept their support. We too often dismiss compliments and encouragement. Don't make that mistake. Embrace it. Seek it out. If you do not have such a cadre of social support, actively begin to acquire one. The best way to acquire social support is to first be supportive of others in any way you can. Your initiatives will earn reciprocity.

- *Self-Control*. Active optimism is enhanced by learning to control yourself, that is, staying calm in the face of adversity, thinking positively, delaying gratification, controlling impulsive urges, and developing your physical well-being.

Let's take a closer look to see how Bandura's four modes of acquisition can be applied as prescriptions to achieve active optimism in your life.

Rx 1: Harness the Power of Optimism and the Self-Fulfilling Prophecy

Your optimism increases with each success you have. You must program yourself to be successful. The mistake that most people make is to choose a challenge that is initially too difficult to manage. There are four ways you can leverage the success-building model in this first prescription:

1. *Break down large tasks into smaller and more manageable parts.* Focus on and complete each small task one at a time. This will make completing the task successfully both much easier and more likely.

2. *When a task is too big for you to manage, ask for assistance.* Delegate as much as is reasonable. Delegation is one of the greatest strengths of successful leaders. It's a force multiplier. And remember, asking for help when you need it is a sign of self-confidence and personal strength, not weakness.

3. *Rehearse your responses.* Psychologists have long known that rehearsal increases the likelihood of success. Rehearsal can be either physical or mental. Whenever possible, practice, practice, practice. Anticipate the most challenging aspects of a task and rehearse your response and solutions. Anticipate your greatest vulnerabilities and devise tactics that avoid or minimize any negative potential outcome. Politicians are often taught to prepare their message for interviews and respond with that message regardless of the questions actually asked. In these cases the politician is not interested in answering the questions to the interviewer's satisfaction. Rather, by having practiced and stayed on message, the politician succeeds in both avoiding uncomfortable topics and hammering the message he wants to convey.

4. *Visualize your successes.* Elite athletes are taught to visualize being successful at whatever they attempt. Golfers, for example, typically visualize a successful shot before they actu-

ally strike the ball. "Imagine where you will be and it will be so," said General Maximus to his troops in the movie *The Gladiator*.

HOMEWORK

Pick one thing you can do, starting next Monday, that will help you begin to develop your active optimism using one or more of the four methods of leveraging the success-building model. Write it here:

_____

_____

_____

Now send yourself an email as a reminder.

Rx 2: Build Active Optimism Vicariously

We believe the best way to build active optimism is by first having success and then applying a self-fulfilling prophecy based on that success. But there's another road to achieving active optimism in the absence of your own success: Watch others be successful at what you want to achieve.

The key is that you must perceive those you observe as either being somehow similar to you or possessing a key to success that you are realistically capable of acquiring.

For example, it won't help basketball players who are six feet tall to watch players who are seven feet tall being successful. Rather, they should watch other six-footers attain success. And it serves little purpose to try to motivate students who graduated from an overcrowded high school with examples of students who graduated from elite private high schools with small classes and individualized attention. Rather, one should hold up as examples students who went on to elite colleges from other overcrowded high schools.

Becoming a member of a group, team, organization, or even a community that is successful is another way to develop active optimism. This happens in all walks of life.

Members of the Johns Hopkins University faculty work daily with the expectation that they will make significant contributions to science. Members of the New York Yankees begin every season with the expectation that they will win a World Series. Students in selective high schools expect to go to selective colleges. Similarly, students at selective colleges expect that they will be successful beyond school, in life in general. Navy SEALs expect to prevail in warfare because they earned acceptance into an elite group of warriors, and in that process they adopted the group's values and cultivated their own personal desire to sustain the legacy of success that the SEALs represent.

With some anxiety, a student entered his first class at Harvard University. The course was known to be difficult. The world-renowned professor—who was considered demanding—entered the class and simply stared at the students for what seemed to be an eternity. Finally, the professor spoke.

"I want you to look around the room and observe your fellow students," she said. Then she added, "The students in this class will be leaders in their respective fields, wherever you go and whatever you do."

Many of the students left class that day different than when they entered. They looked around the room and saw people just like themselves who were going to excel. "If they can do it, I can!"

one student thought to himself. Students left the classroom with an expectation of success that would extend far beyond that classroom, and, oh yes, they left with the expectation that they had a 350-year legacy to uphold as well. No doubt that was the professor's intention.

———

The pitcher on the mound, still in his early 20s, was about to pitch in a spring training baseball game for the New York Yankees, arguably the most iconic sports team in the world. During his warm-up pitches, he was having trouble throwing strikes. At that moment, a famous player, destined to be in baseball's Hall of Fame, approached the pitcher's mound from center field. He said simply, "You're a Yankee now, so pitch like it!"

———

Members of successful groups at any level in any endeavor tend to be successful, in part, because of the expectation of success that group membership bestows and reinforces. Unfortunately, the opposite is also true. Members of unsuccessful groups often have great challenges to overcome.

Here are three things you can do to increase your active optimism vicariously:

- Join interest groups, clubs, and even sports teams that will allow you to observe how more skillful individuals function. Once you achieve their level of competence through observation and practice, you'll need to join a more challenging group to obtain the vicarious benefits of learning from those more accomplished than yourself.
- Attend public readings, speeches, and performances that relate to the skills you want to acquire.

- Read as many books and articles as you can on people who have achieved success in areas in which you want to succeed. If possible, write to them or call them for an interview. Try to discover their keys to success.

HOMEWORK

Pick one thing you can do, starting next Monday, that will help you begin to develop active optimism via vicarious success using one or more of these prescriptions. Write it here:

_____

_____

_____

Now send yourself an email as a reminder.

Rx 3: Build Active Optimism Through the Encouragement and Support of Others

Active optimism can also be developed from the active encouragement and support of others. Evidence suggests that interpersonal connectedness and support are powerful determinants of resilience. In the military, unit cohesion is critical. In the social and business worlds, sometimes it really is whom you know that counts, and the strength of the bonds of affinity. The benefits of interpersonal support have been known for over a century. Charles Darwin, writing in 1871, noted that a tribe whose members were always ready to aid one another and make sacrifices for the common good would be victorious over most other tribes. This certainly applies to teams—whether social, corporate, or athletic.

JIM CRAIG, 1980 "MIRACLE ON ICE" OLYMPIC TEAM

Abbey-Robin Tillery dared to dream. Against the odds, she dreamed that there was something better. Jim Craig (born May 31, 1957) dared to dream as well. He and his American teammates dreamed of winning an Olympic gold medal in ice hockey at a time when such a thing was deemed impossible. Craig, the goaltender for what turned out to be the gold-medal winning 1980 U.S. Olympic ice hockey team, was the face of one of the most iconic moments in American sports history.

Craig was one of eight children in a family in North Easton, Massachusetts. After playing hockey for one year at Massasoit Community College, he transferred to Boston University, where he also played hockey. In 1978, his Boston University team won the NCAA championship. He was then selected to be the starting goalie for the 1980 Olympics team.

The greatest power in the ice hockey world at that time was the Soviet Union. It was a team of seasoned athletes who would routinely play and routinely defeat the best professional ice hockey teams in the world. Between 1954 and 1991, the Soviet team won seven of nine Olympic gold medals and 18 world championships.

In a semifinal game on February 22, 1980, in Lake Placid, New York, the U.S. team faced the Soviets, who were the heavy favorites to win another gold medal. The Soviets scored the first goal of the game, and many thought an inevitable defeat had begun. The Soviets took 39 shots on goal compared to the U.S. team's 16.

Nevertheless, at the game-ending buzzer, the American team prevailed by the score of 4–3. With three seconds to play in the game, ABC sportscaster Al Michaels' now iconic rhetorical question—"Do you believe in miracles?"—was seared into the minds of all who watched and listened. The American victory would thereafter be known as "The Miracle on Ice." That victory was selected the top sports moment of the 20th century by *Sports Illustrated* magazine.

Two days after defeating the Soviet Union, the Americans would defeat Finland 4–2 and win the gold medal. Craig was credited with being the anchoring force of the Olympic victory.

Immediately following the Olympics, Craig joined the professional National Hockey League, playing for the Atlanta Flames. The next year he was traded to the Boston Bruins, and he ended his career playing for the Minnesota North Stars. Craig played in 30 professional games over three seasons ending in 1984.

The success Craig enjoyed as an Olympian did not directly translate to success in the NHL, nor to the business world. Craig had to reinvent himself. He did so based on core attributes and actions. Today, Craig is the author of the book *Gold Medal Strategies* and president of Gold Medal Strategies, a successful marketing and promotions firm. He says his goal is to help others develop the attitudes that will help them realize their dreams.

Dream! But to realize your dream, share it with others. To realize your dreams, the support of others can be critical. "You must learn to tell others about your dreams," Craig told us. "Discuss your dreams. If you get someone to believe in you, someone to teach you things, you can do great things. Herb Brooks was our Olympic team coach. Brooks was pulling greatness from people, holding us accountable. We weren't the dream team but a 'team of dreamers.' If you don't tell people your dreams then they can't help you achieve them. Make sure you fill your life with the proper influencers and mentors to guide you and help pull greatness out of you. Whether it is discipline, confidence, or courage you need, surround yourself with positive influences."

When considering his fondest moments of the 1980 Olympics, Craig says:

"The lasting memory is how unselfish all the players on the team really were and how committed they were. The overall dream of winning a gold medal was more important than anything we accomplished as individuals. I'm still proud to be part of that team."

In order to increase your degree of connectedness:

- Find a group with shared interests. It will soon become a support system. Show interest in the things that interest others. Most will be eager to share their knowledge and enthusiasm.
- If you do not have a mentor or an informal adviser, try to find one. Beyond family, however, such support must be earned. Ask if you can shadow someone professionally. Volunteer to assist in activities that may exceed your current responsibilities. Ask for nothing in return other than the

privilege of learning. You will be surprised how much such an investment actually returns. If nothing else, the people you ask will certainly remember you.

- Interpersonal support says someone has your back. In the military it is commonly agreed that on the battlefield, no one will be left behind. Leave no one behind and you will never find yourself alone. We will discuss these concepts in far more detail later in this book.

HOMEWORK

Pick one thing you can do, starting next Monday, that will help you begin to develop active optimism via interpersonal support using one or more of these prescriptions. Write it here:

_____

_____

_____

Now send yourself an email as a reminder.

Rx 4: Build Active Optimism Through Self-Control

Have you ever seen someone experience an anxiety attack? Have you ever experienced an anxiety attack yourself? Most occur because people are afraid of losing control. At the first sign of distress, a person begins saying catastrophic things, such as, "I'm losing control. . . . I am going to panic. . . . It's going to be terrible. . . . I'm going to die!" As the person engages in these catastrophic thoughts, greater and greater physical and psychological distress occur. Soon the catastrophic thoughts become a self-fulfilling prophecy, and a full-blown panic attack ensues, though very seldom does one die because of a panic attack.

The ability to control oneself becomes a powerful determinant of subsequent behavior. When you can control your actions, thoughts, and even bodily reactions, it conveys self-confidence and active optimism. Your ability to delay impulsive actions will prevent overreacting. If you can interpret an increased heart rate as positive preparation for action, rather than as the first step into an abyss of panic, you can prevent catastrophic physical and psychological escalations. Learning how to control both self-defeating thoughts and overarousal can be powerful sources of active optimism.

Biologic feedback, or biofeedback, is a therapy developed in the 1960s and practiced extensively through the 1990s. It consists of using electronic monitors to measure muscle tension and brain-wave activity. Thanks to this technology, patients themselves and not just their physicians observe the instantaneous activity of muscles or brain waves.

Researchers learned that with experience, patients could actually control the muscle activity associated with headaches, muscle spasm, and some brain activity that seems associated with relaxation and even hyperactivity syndromes. Today, biofeedback is being investigated in the treatment of depression, headaches, chronic pain, high blood pressure, Raynaud's disease and urinary incontinence.

A particularly interesting aspect of biofeedback therapy is that regardless of the physiological activity that patients were learning to control, patients invariably voiced improved self-confidence and self-esteem. They had learned to control something they thought they couldn't, and it seemed to apply to all aspects of life. And because of this improved sense of control, a sense of calm ensued. One patient noted, "The things that used to bother me just don't bother me anymore."

Here are some ways you can enhance your self-control to increase your active optimism:

- Recognize your physical early warning signs of distress and act as soon as possible to reduce them. **Make a list here of your early warning signs of distress:**

  _____

  _____

  _____

  _____

- Use a relaxation or calming technique. For example, take breaths deep enough so that when you inhale your stomach expands. Inhale for about two seconds and then immediately (do not hold your breath) exhale for three seconds. Repeat this two times, but do not breathe so deeply that you feel light-headed. This simple diaphragmatic breathing is a very rapid and effective technique for establishing a sense of calm and control. (Elite snipers are taught to visualize the target, take a deep breath, exhale, and squeeze the trigger.)

- Delay important decisions until you've had a chance to consider your options. The best way to avoid an impulsive mistake is to delay making what may be an impulsive decision. If the urgency you feel is mostly self-imposed, then delay important decisions until you've had a chance to consider your options. Interestingly, the ability to resist the temptations of urgency is itself a form of self-control.

HOMEWORK

Pick one thing you can do, starting next Monday, that will help you begin to develop active optimism via self-control using one or more of these prescriptions. Write it here:

Now send yourself an email as a reminder.

KEY POINTS TO REMEMBER ABOUT ACTIVE OPTIMISM

- There are two types of optimism: active and passive. Active optimism is the deeply held belief that you can act in a meaningful way and make a difference as an agent of change. Most people possess the passive version. Navy SEALs and other extraordinary people possess the active version.
- Research strongly suggests that active optimism can be increased at any age simply by employing one or more of the following tactics:
    —Do things successfully. When necessary, break down tasks into smaller parts. Delegate when you can, and harness the self-fulfilling prophecy "Imagine where you will be and it will be so."
    —Watch others being successful.
    —Give and seek coaching, encouragement and, support.
    —Exercise self-control.
- Remember the SEAL Ethos: "In the worst of conditions . . . I will not fail."

Now look back at your self-assessment. Let's see what type of optimist you might be. If you scored highly (Strongly Agree) on item #1, "I am truly thankful for the positive things in life," it suggests that you look back with appreciation, but it says nothing about looking forward. If you scored highly on items #2 and #3, "I hope that my life will be happy and rewarding" and "I expect life to be positive and rewarding," it suggests a passive optimism. However, if you scored highly on items #4 and #5, "I do not wait for good things to happen, I make them happen," and "When I encounter challenges and even failures, I know I will be successful in time," it suggests a high level of active optimism. This is the highest level of optimism reflected in this self-assessment.

CHAPTER 2

THE COURAGE TO BE DECISIVE AND TAKE PERSONAL RESPONSIBILITY

In the absence of orders I will take charge, lead my teammates, and accomplish the mission. I stand ready to bring the full spectrum of . . . power to bear in order to achieve my mission and the goals established. . . . The execution of my duties will be swift . . . yet guided by the very principles I serve to defend. By wearing the Trident, I accept the responsibility of my chosen profession and way of life.

—Adapted from the U.S. Navy SEAL Ethos

Resilience is the ability to personally rebound from adversity. When we speak of having the courage to be decisive in the context of resilience, we really mean the ability to effectively narrow a myriad of options and make the difficult decision to take action in the wake of adversity or in the face of extraordinary challenges.

In Chapter One, we discussed active optimism as the first of our five factors of personal resilience. An attitude of optimism alone, however, will not create a resiliency advantage. It will not bring you back from the abyss. As the German writer Johann Wolfgang von Goethe (1749–1832) noted, "Knowing is not enough; we must apply. Willing is not enough; we must do." The American humorist Will Rogers (1879–1935) not only recognized the importance of decisiveness but also pointed to the risks associated with a lack of action. He once opined, "Even if you are on the right track, you will get run over if you just sit there."

SELF-ASSESSMENT #2

Directions: Circle the answer that best describes how strongly you agree with the following statements.

1. *I prefer to make difficult decisions rather than have someone else make them for me.*
    1—Strongly disagree
    2—Disagree
    3—Agree
    4—Strongly agree

2. *For me, making difficult decisions has usually been relatively easy.*
    1—Strongly disagree
    2—Disagree
    3—Agree
    4—Strongly agree

3. *Many people view me as a decisive person.*

    1—Strongly disagree

    2—Disagree

    3—Agree

    4—Strongly agree

4. *Many people view me as a prudent risk taker.*

    1—Strongly disagree

    2—Disagree

    3—Agree

    4—Strongly agree

5. *Anything worth having is worth failing for.*

    1—Strongly disagree

    2—Disagree

    3—Agree

    4—Strongly agree

This self-assessment is not a clinical diagnostic tool. It is simply a survey designed to motivate you to think about your attitudes concerning decisiveness and personal responsibility. When you have completed the survey, simply add up the numbers next to the answers you have circled for items #1–5. The higher your score the better, as it suggests you are inclined to be decisive. Take this self-assessment periodically to see how you are doing. Now let's take a closer look at decisive action and personal responsibility and why they convey a resiliency advantage.

Here in Chapter Two, we'll look at the fundamental elements

of decisiveness as well as accepting personal responsibility for the
decisions you make.

THE POWER OF DECISIVENESS AND
TAKING RESPONSIBILITY

The decision to be not only a survivor but a victor in the wake of
adversity allows you to put your foot on the first rung of the ladder
that will begin your ascent out of the abyss. For many, taking decisive action and then accepting personal responsibility for decisions
are self-evident virtues. What might not be self-evident is why.
Decisive action appears to be capable of (1) mitigating adversity,
(2) helping you rebound from adversity, and (3) promoting growth
in the wake of adversity.

Decisiveness Mitigates Adversity

The great Chinese military strategist Sun Tzu over 2,000 years ago
wrote in *The Art of War* that decisive action is a virtue. He noted
that vacillation saps the strength of any army. It wastes valuable
resources. Thus, he concluded that if action is necessary, make it
swift, act boldly, because no one benefits from protracted conflict
or ambivalent leadership.

Think about your own life. Have you ever wasted valuable
time, money, or energy because you were unsure what to do? Have
you ever waited so long trying to make a decision that the opportunity itself was lost?

So how does decisiveness help you? Those who are first to act
most often reap the rewards that life has to offer. The saying "The
early bird catches the worm" refers not only to early risers but also

to those who are first to act. Opportunities in life seem to benefit those who *act* upon them more than those who merely recognize them.

We know that the decision to have yearly medical examinations matters. Early diagnosis of a wide variety of medical conditions reduces the subsequent complexity and cost of treatment. And, in the case of potentially life-threatening disease, early action dramatically increases preservation of life itself.

In the cases of breast cancer and colon cancer, the decision to participate in screening procedures can lead to the early detection of precancerous neoplasms and even the early detection of cancer itself. Treatment of the cancer before it spreads yields highly favorable outcomes. In the case of colon cancer, early detection, while it is still within the intestine wall, leads to cure rates approaching 100 percent, according to a 2008 report of the U.S. Centers for Disease Control and Prevention. The David Drew Clinic, a preventive medicine clinic in Maryland that emphasizes screening and early detection, reports that in the 45-to-65-year age group, the mortality rate for its patients from all diseases is 1 percent, compared to the national average of 14 percent.

From another perspective, we understand that decisiveness in war often wins battles, whereas hesitancy often leads to defeat. Take, for example, the actions of Winston Churchill in the early days of World War II.

On May 10, 1940, military forces of Adolf Hitler's Germany began an invasion of France and its surrounding countries. Germany had 136 divisions. The Allied forces (French, British, and Belgian) together had only 126 divisions, but almost 1,000 more tanks than the Germans. The French armies were taken by surprise and began a retreat on May 14. Although the battle was far from over, French Prime Minister Paul Reynaud telephoned British Prime Minister Churchill on May 15 and famously said, "We have been defeated. We are beaten; we have lost the battle."

Despite Churchill's encouragement that the battle had just begun, a substantial counterattack wasn't initiated until May 25, but it was too late to be effective. The German army reached the coast of France largely unhindered, isolating the Allied forces to the north. As the Germans moved north to destroy the remaining Allied armies, Churchill ordered an evacuation of British forces from the area around Dunkirk, France.

In what must have been a remarkably difficult decision to make, Churchill ordered the wounded soldiers to be evacuated last. His reasoning was that Britain first and foremost needed able-bodied soldiers if the German army decided to attack Great Britain. Ultimately, more than 300,000 troops were evacuated from Dunkirk to fight another day. The adverse effects of Germany's invasion of France had been mitigated by Churchill's bold and initially counterintuitive actions as the typical convention in war was to evacuate the wounded first.

In the wake of their military defeat, the French ultimately replaced Reynaud and installed the Vichy government, which was friendly to Hitler's Germany. Part of the arrangement was that the French naval fleet could be subject to German influence. Once again, Churchill had to make a difficult decision. He could not allow French warships to be used against Britain.

On July 3, 1940, British warships surrounded the French fleet at the port of Mers-el-Kébir, outside Oran, Algeria. Churchill gave the French commanders the option of disabling their ships so they could not be used against Britain, surrendering their ships altogether, or sailing to a neutral port until the end of the war. The

French commanders, insisting they would never allow the Germans to use their ships against Britain, failed to comply with Churchill's demands. In the meantime, in a move that seemed contrary to the French captains' assurances, the Vichy government sent reinforcements to Oran.

Consequently, Churchill ordered an attack on Britain's allies, the French fleet. More than 1,200 French sailors were killed. It is said that Churchill wept as he informed the British House of Commons. Upon hearing of the prime minister's decisive actions in the wake of the military defeat that preceded Dunkirk, the members of the House gave Churchill a standing ovation. It was clear that Britain was united and would be resilient in the shadow of tragedy.

In business, being decisive often leads to creating trends rather than following them. A visionary trendsetter, Steve Jobs was once referred to as the "Father of the Digital Revolution." Jobs, who co-founded Apple Computer Inc. with Steve Wozniak in 1976, shaped the fields of computing, personal-communications devices, music, and modern movie-making. But his greatest strength was his ability to make a decision and follow it through to fruition.

Wozniak was the true technical genius of Apple computing. But Jobs was the driving force behind the ascent of Apple products and related ventures such as Pixar, the digital-movie company. His ability to understand future markets, think beyond current limitations, create nontraditional business models, assemble a team of technical experts, and guide (some would say push) the company to creative excellence is what really made Apple (and almost everything else that Jobs touched) successful, according to Jobs's biographer Walter Isaacson.

At a Macworld conference, Jobs once said, "There's an old Wayne Gretzky quote that I love: 'I skate to where the puck is going to be, not where it has been.' And we've always tried to do that at Apple. Since the very, very beginning. And we always will."

While Jobs was quick to see opportunities, he was also quick to see projects with little potential. He terminated a number of projects, such as the OpenDoc document management system and Newton, a personal digital assistant in which the former Apple CEO had invested over $100 million. In a 1994 PBS interview, Jobs said:

> The minute that you understand that you can poke life and . . . something will pop out the other side, that you can change it, you can mold it. That's maybe the most important thing. It's to shake off this erroneous notion that life is there and you're just gonna live in it, versus embrace it, change it, improve it, make your mark upon it. Once you learn that, you'll never be the same again.

In 1997 Apple launched a new slogan that sums up the approach Steve Jobs took to business and to life: "Think Different."

Decisiveness and responsibility even mitigate the adverse effects of aging. In a series of highly regarded studies, Harvard professor Ellen Langer and her colleagues found that decisiveness and increased personal responsibility were associated with positive health outcomes, including longer life.

In a study of nursing home residents conducted by researchers Langer and Judith Rodin in 1976, one group was provided an environment in which responsibility and decision making were fostered. This group was also given the option of caring for a plant and the chance to decide on which of two nights to watch a movie.

A second group received communications that made more explicit the policy of the nursing home that it was the staff's responsibility to care for them. Moreover, these residents were implicitly denied choice: They weren't given the option of caring for a plant, and they were assigned a specific night to view a movie.

Three weeks after the environmental alterations, the residents who had been given an enhanced sense of decision making, responsibility, and choice were more active and alert, felt happier, and became more involved in a variety of activities than the comparison group.

Rodin and Langer returned to the nursing home 18 months later and found that residents in the responsibility group remained more active, sociable, vigorous, and self-initiating than the comparison or control groups. Moreover, during this 18-month period, the responsibility-induced group showed a significantly greater increase in general health than the comparison participants. In fact, only 15 percent of the responsibility-induced group died within this time, compared with 30 percent of the comparison group.

Decisiveness Helps You Rebound from Adversity

Decisiveness not only helps you mitigate adversity, but it seems to aid people in rebounding from adversity. Depression and feelings of hopelessness often follow in the wake of hardship. Psychologists have long known that if these feelings are allowed to persist, they can become paralyzing forces that dramatically reduce the likelihood of resilience.

Take the case of posttraumatic stress disorder (PTSD), by definition a syndrome of stress reactions that sometimes occurs after one has been exposed to a life-threatening situation (trauma). Its symptoms include unrelenting thoughts of the event, depression, anxiety, sleep disturbance, anger, and even inclinations toward violence.

PTSD is the most severe psychiatric disorder that affects otherwise healthy people. Psychiatrist Frank Ochberg made the early observation that the longer one waits to address the symptoms of PTSD, the harder it might become to ultimately treat it. His explanation for this phenomenon was that people exposed to traumatic events develop a "trauma membrane" that serves as a protective barrier to reduce further injury. This psychological shield shows up as the desire to withdraw from social contact, even from one's family, combined with an emotional numbing. There are numerous cases of Vietnam veterans who retreated to forests of the northwest United States and became reclusive as a means of shielding themselves from further human contact.

The problem, of course, is that while the trauma membrane serves to protect from further psychological injury, it also serves as a barrier, inhibiting the healing support of others such as friends and family. At the same time, the membrane reinforces psychological paralysis, making it very challenging to overcome psychological inertia. It even serves as a deterrent to seeking psychological treatment.

Conversely, acting quickly and decisively has been shown to be of benefit in reducing stress and empowering people to rebound from adversity. The most powerful way of helping yourself in the wake of adversity appears to be resisting the pressures of psychological avoidance and paralysis by doing something to help yourself or others. Take action. Gain strength by identifying and actively pursuing a goal.

Taking that first step is empowering and tends to result in other successes. To borrow from the principles of physics, an object in motion tends to remain in motion, and an object at rest tends to remain at rest. As mentioned in Chapter One, Albert Bandura has concluded, after 40 years of research, that the single best way to promote self-esteem, self-empowerment, and resilience is through achievement.

In his critically acclaimed book *The Optimistic Child*, psychologist Martin E. P. Seligman argues, "Our society has changed from an achieving society to a feel-good society. Up until the 1960s, achievement was the most important goal to instill in our children. This goal was overtaken by the twin goals of happiness and self-esteem."

Now you might read this and ask, "What's wrong with happiness and self-esteem?" The answer is, nothing, as long as they are built on a foundation of something more substantial than the mere desire to possess them or to give them to others. Seligman argues that we cannot directly teach lasting self-esteem to our children. Rather he says, "Self-esteem is caused by . . . successes and failures in the world." Self-esteem is earned, not given. What we need, he says, "is not children who are encouraged to feel good, but children who are taught the skills of doing well."

Decisiveness Promotes Growth in the Wake of Adversity

So far we have seen that decisive action mitigates adversity's effects and aids in rebounding from it. In this section, we shall show how decisive action can actually promote growth.

We've recently learned that in the process of bouncing back from adversity, you can not only completely recover, but you can become stronger and happier than you were before the adversity ever occurred. The German philosopher Friedrich Nietzsche (1844–1900), writing in his 1888 *Twilight of the Idols*, declared, "What does not kill me makes me stronger." There is now evidence that Nietzsche was indeed correct.

The terms that are often used to capture this notion of growth after adversity are *transformative stress* or *posttraumatic growth*. This type of transformative stress, as noted earlier, is not simply a return to baseline but an improvement. Those who experience transformative stress report a sense of personal empowerment, greater appreciation of life, greater optimism, greater appreciation of interpersonal relationships, and sometimes a dramatic change in life's priorities in the wake of adversity. They reconsider what's really important in life.

GEORGE MASI

George Masi is executive vice president and chief operating officer of Harris Health System in Houston, Texas, the third-largest public hospital and health system in the nation. Comprising three teaching hospitals and 17 large community clinics, the health system is affiliated with two medical schools, staffed by 8,500 personnel, and has an annual operating budget in excess of $1.3 billion.

Masi's entire 40-year professional career has been in healthcare administration. He learned many lessons about resilience, leadership, and life along the way, especially during his 27 years as a commissioned officer in the U.S. Army. Masi retired as a colonel, having commanded medical units at the company, battalion, and hospital levels.

"A situation in my professional life that most exemplifies how resiliency sustained me when confronted with adversity occurred when I was a young captain, serving as a medical company commander in the 194th Armored Brigade garrisoned at Fort Knox, Kentucky," he told us.

In January 1980, Masi had just completed the Army Medical Department Officer Advanced Course en route to assuming his first company command. He was assigned to Fort Knox, where he assumed command of Bravo Company in the 194th Armored Brigade. For a young army officer, company command is an early predictor of career potential. The unspoken rule is: Do well in company command and you will likely compete favorably for advanced schooling and promotion to major. Anything less may spell an early end to one's budding army career.

Shortly after Masi took command, the 194th Armored Brigade, which at the time was the largest separate combat brigade in the army, deployed on a major field-training exercise named Operation Winter Fox. The exercise was designed to test the brigade's preparedness for combat operations. Bravo Company was the only tactical medical unit in the brigade. According to Masi, Army tank commanders typically know little about the details of medical support, except that when it's needed, it had better be there. With no higher medical headquarters in the brigade to rely on for command, control, or guidance, Bravo Company was on its own.

Unfortunately for Masi, Bravo Company had not been deployed to its full capability in far too long. The unit was well prepared for conducting sick call and other routine garrison missions, but deployment to the field environment and providing healthcare during tactical field maneuvers was another matter.

Adding to Masi's problems, most of Bravo Company's complex field medical equipment had been kept in storage. Communication gear, vital in any tactical environment, was rarely fully tested. Because the unit's field medical equipment had never been fully engaged, field generators had rarely, if ever, been run to full power. The simple reality was that Bravo Company was unprepared to deploy and accomplish its tactical medical mission.

Against the objections of his first sergeant and his young lieutenants, Masi decided that Bravo Company would deploy and fully activate all of its field medical capability during Operation Winter Fox. Masi stated the results were nothing short of "catastrophic." Having convoyed to the field site, it was clear that the soldiers of Bravo Company had little understanding of how to set up and operate the field medical equipment, nor were they able to correctly deploy the requisite tents, medical equipment, radios, and generator stations.

The story of Bravo Company's disaster quickly spread to the brigade headquarters. It wasn't long before the brigade commander appeared on-site to see for himself. By all indications, Masi's army career seemed to be ending before it even began.

In the most devastating of possible outcomes, for Masi and Bravo Company alike, the brigade's executive officer urged that Masi order his company to stand down and return to the garrison. Masi refused. In his words, "I respectfully declined to do so even at the risk of being relieved of my command. Instead, after the brigade's leadership departed, I chose to address the soldiers of Bravo Company and describe the reality of our situation."

According to Masi, the failure of previous leadership to train the unit to maximum capacity had left his soldiers unprepared to accomplish the mission.

"Rather than stand Bravo Company down," he said, "we remained in the field for the duration of the brigade exercise. I asked for and was given permission by the brigade headquarters to disengage Bravo Company from the larger exercise, but to remain in the field until Operation Winter Fox concluded. I decided we would use this time to relentlessly train on the basics. We would learn from our mistakes.

"We practiced medical-site deployment and convoy operations, setting up the field medical site, breaking it down, packing the equipment, and convoying again. We trained day and night for two solid weeks. We did not stop there. When we returned to garrison, we planned and executed modular training events, with each squad and section deploying their equipment and training to standard on that equipment. Then we graduated to collective training where we deployed the entire medical company with all of its equipment. We repeated this training cycle over and over again. We became very proficient."

Months later, in March 1982, the 194th Armored Brigade found itself in the high desert of Fort Irwin, California's National Training Center. The brigade was participating in a massive army, air force, and marine corps joint training exercise, Operation Gallant Eagle. The exercise, which included the 82nd Airborne Division, featured land and air operations in what was at the time the largest peacetime airborne parachute airdrop ever made by the U.S. military.

The morning of the drop, however, things went terribly wrong. Masi described the situation:

"It was six a.m. and the sun had just risen when a huge squadron of Air Force C-130 and C-141 Starlifter aircraft appeared over the Mojave Desert some 130 miles northeast of Los Angeles. From the landing zones on the desert floor, plumes of colored smoke rose identifying the jump zones and the wind direction. At the go-ahead signal, given by ground spotters, the sky came alive with parachutes.

"But unexpected high winds blew in just as thousands of paratroopers began their exits from the aircraft. Ground wind gusts of up to 20 miles per hour caught many of the paratroopers' chutes as they were about to land and dragged them for long distances across the desert floor and across a rocky terrain. As they were dragged along the desert floor, many of the paratroopers were unable to release their safety catches to disengage their chutes."

There were many casualties—156 injured and several fatalities. A call immediately went out on the field radios for real-world medical support. This was not a training exercise.

Bravo Company responded by redeploying via convoy from its training site to the drop zone. The company's entire medical-treatment facility was set up on-site. The unit medics and physicians expertly treated dozens of paratroopers and medically prepared others for evacuation to higher levels of care. For its efforts, Bravo Company was decorated by the 194th Armored Brigade and recognized by the 82nd Airborne Division.

Masi's story exemplifies tough, courageous decision making. During Operation Winter Fox, when Masi's executive officer suggested that the company stand down in the wake of an operational disaster, Masi risked his career by refusing. And not only did he refuse, but he attacked the problem.

He stood before his soldiers and explained that through no fault of their own, they were unprepared to deliver the essential medical support the brigade needed. Once he framed the reality of the situation, he planned and had his unit execute training, during the day and night, for the two weeks Bravo Company remained in the field. Upon returning to the garrison, the unit's training continued with the ultimate goal of being able to successfully deploy in the field with full tactical capability.

Now, let's return to Steve Jobs. His success didn't come easily, despite the great immunity to pressure he demonstrated early in his career. In 1985, Jobs was forced to resign from the company he and Wozniak had founded. In a Stanford University commencement address in 2005, Jobs recalled that getting "fired" was one of the best things that ever happened to him.

"The heaviness of being successful was replaced by the lightness of being a beginner again, less sure about everything," he said. "It freed me to enter one of the most creative periods of my life."

Jobs went on to say he was "pretty sure none of this would have happened if I hadn't been fired from Apple. It was awful-tasting medicine, but I guess the patient needed it."

After leaving Apple, Jobs went on to pioneer in arenas previously untouched by Apple, including digital movies. Ironically, when Jobs was fired from Apple in 1985, his net worth was less than $100 million. By the time he died in 2011, it was estimated at over $8 billion, according to biographer Walter Isaacson. As American poet Robert Frost noted, "Freedom lies in being bold."

Bold people making bold decisions have changed the world. One such person is Ben Carson.

BENJAMIN S. CARSON SR., MD

Born in 1951, Ben Carson is one of the world's most accomplished neurosurgeons and true visionaries. He leads a life of decisiveness based upon optimism. His remarkable life has been chronicled in several books and the motion picture *Gifted Hands*.

Carson was raised in a financially impoverished single-parent home in Detroit, Michigan. In his early years, he was plagued with poor grades, a violent temper, and low self-esteem. Despite these early challenges and limitations, Carson rose to the highest echelons at the world's greatest medical institutions. His resiliency was not a matter of luck.

Encouraged by his mother to read at a young age, Carson quickly figured out that knowledge was indeed a source of power, and he developed a passion for it. That passion for knowledge carried him from the academic wastelands to graduation from high school with academic honors in 1969. Carson was admitted to Yale University for undergraduate school and later earned his medical degree at the University of Michigan.

From there he pursued neurosurgery at the Johns Hopkins Medical Institutions. At age 33, he became the director of pediatric neurosurgery and co-director of the Johns Hopkins Craniofacial Center—the youngest major division director in Johns Hopkins history. Upon retiring from active surgery at Hopkins, Carson was appointed professor of neurosurgery, oncology, plastic surgery, and pediatrics, and elected to the National Academy of Sciences Institute of Medicine. In 2008, President George W. Bush awarded Carson the Presidential Medal of Freedom, the United States's highest civilian honor.

During his remarkable tenure at Hopkins, Carson was responsible for performing pioneering surgeries that changed the medical world, but not without risk. His career is a case study in making difficult decisions based on undaunted optimism.

In 1985, Carson successfully performed a controversial and dangerous hemispherectomy (removal of a portion of the outer part of the brain) on a child who suffered from intractable seizures. The technique, although used 40 years earlier, had fallen into disrepute. Undaunted by the failures of others, Carson completed the surgery, giving the patient her life back.

From then on, he was internationally famous. In 1986, he pioneered a radical intrauterine surgical procedure to relieve fluid-related pressure on the brain of an unborn child. In 1987, Carson was contacted by the parents of seven-month-old occipital craniopagus conjoined twins (sometimes called Siamese twins) from Germany. Patrick and Benjamin Binder were born joined at the head. Because the boys were joined at the back of their heads, and because they had separate functional brains, Carson was optimistic that surgery to separate them could be performed. The major problem during such surgeries is that the patients often lose great quantities of blood, which often leads to death.

Carson consulted with a cardiac surgeon and decided to employ a technique known as hypothermic arrest. The patients' bodies would be cooled in order to reduce cranial blood flow and minimize blood loss. The 70-member surgical team, led by Carson, worked for 22 hours. At the end, the twins were successfully separated and capable of living independent lives. Carson's success was particularly noteworthy because it was the first time occipital conjoined twins had been separated with both babies surviving.

In 1994, Carson traveled to South Africa to separate another set of conjoined twins. This time the outcome was devastating: Both children died. Despite this failure, in 1997, Carson and his team traveled to Zambia to separate infant boys Luka and Joseph Banda. This operation was difficult because the patients were vertical craniopagus twins—joined at the tops of their heads. Previous attempts at this form of surgery had ended in failure.

Carson's unfailing optimism allowed him to accept the challenge that others would not have attempted. After a 28-hour operation, both boys survived, and neither suffered brain damage. Had Carson given up after the unsuccessful surgery in 1994, the Banda twins would not have been able to live separate lives.

Despite a decade of unparalleled successes, in 2003, failure struck Carson again. Carson and his 100-person team attempted to separate Ladan and Laleh Bijani, two 29-year-old adult twins from Iraq. The surgery lasted 52 hours. Sadly, both patients died soon after the separation. Though unsuccessful, this was the first attempt to separate adult occipital conjoined twins. The failure did not deter Carson, who remained optimistic that he could continue to make a difference. And he did, achieving a long series of visionary breakthroughs.

In 2002, Carson faced his own medical challenge: He was diagnosed with prostate cancer. He underwent a successful surgery, and he continues to attempt to change the world, now through philanthropic and political initiatives.

What can we learn about human resiliency by looking at the amazing life of Ben Carson, MD? He believes in self-determination for individuals, communities, and nations. He has said that optimism is essential to rebounding from adversity. But optimism isn't enough. Armed with optimism, you must then have the courage to act, to take risks. Carson noted that there is no such thing as an average person.

"If you have a normal brain, you can become superior," he said. "What happens with your life is up to you. Growing up, when I read books about successful people, I found out many that didn't start out that way. I began to understand it's not the environment, it's you and your attitude.

"I hated poverty growing up; then I realized it was a

choice. You can work hard and achieve whatever you want. I ignored the pessimists from the time I was a teenager throughout my entire career. My adviser wanted me to drop out of medical school. When I started performing surgical procedures that others had failed to perform or that had never been tried before, people said, 'You can't do that.' Previously, 70 percent of dwarfs would die because their brain stem was being crushed by bone at the stem of their skull. We devised a way to fix it. Others were actually outraged, basing their opinion on unsuccessful cases in the past.

"Because of our successes, procedures are now being done routinely all over the world. If you use intellect then you can learn from what has happened in the past and from what others are doing and then you can move much faster."

Carson made two pivotal decisions that caused his life to take a resilient trajectory. The first was to gain the power to change through the acquisition of knowledge. The second was the decision to gain control over his emotional life.

"I had an incredibly horrible temper," he said. "And I did get into fights; I would injure people. I would just become irrational because I would get so angry.

"As far as the stabbing, I was already an 'A' student at that point. Another youngster angered me, I had a large camping knife, and I tried to stab him in the abdomen. Fortunately he had on a large metal belt buckle under his clothing, and the knife blade struck with such force that it broke and he fled in terror. But I was more terrified as I recognized that I was trying to kill somebody over nothing.

"Because of the stabbing incident, I locked myself in the bathroom; read the Bible, Proverbs. It's a habit I maintained from that day to present. You don't get anywhere kicking down the door or punching someone in the face. It's selfish and you really don't have control.

"I came to understand that when you react like that, it actually is a sign of weakness because it means that other people and the environment can control you, and I decided that I didn't want to be that easily controlled. And I've never had another problem with temper since that day. I let go of anger, and I have control because my opponents can't make me angry."

When discussing the source of his resilience, Carson noted: "It came from my mother. She refused to be a victim. She taught me to not be a victim. She was one of 24 children; she had a third-grade education, unable to get good jobs. Despite all of that, she never felt sorry for herself and she never felt sorry for us. She said, 'Do you have a brain? Then it doesn't matter what others are doing. You don't have to be one of the crowd.' I became the brain surgeon, and my brother became the rocket scientist."

THE HALO EFFECT

But wait, there's more. Decisiveness, as we have implied, is a rare commodity. So rare that those who are viewed positively because of their decisiveness will tend to be viewed positively in other aspects of their life. Thus, positive regard that others hold for you because you are decisive tends to literally bias their view of you in other aspects of your life.

This cognitive or perceptual bias is called the "halo effect." Educational psychologist Edward Lee Thorndike coined the term in the early 1900s to describe the cognitive perceptual bias in which people who possess attributes that others desire but do not possess, such as decisiveness, are perceived as attractive, courageous, strong and/or unusually competent, or successful.

Most people struggle making difficult decisions. We commonly fall prey to paralysis by analysis, loathing to act until we've analyzed all the relevant data. Or we're simply afraid to risk a poor outcome. As American author and psychotherapist Virginia Satir once noted, "Most people prefer the certainty of misery to the misery of uncertainty." We recognize that failing in ourselves and marvel at those who are capable of making difficult decisions. We bestow upon those who are decisive not only our admiration, but the expectation that they can do almost everything well. So if you can be extraordinarily decisive when others cannot, you are likely to become the beneficiary of the halo effect and be seen as extraordinary in other ways.

Once you become the beneficiary of the halo effect, you may then begin to view yourself in a more positive light. Thus, the halo effect may then evolve into a self-fulfilling prophecy! Armed with the cognitive bias of the halo effect and the power of the self-fulfilling prophecy, who knows how far you can go?

TAKING RESPONSIBILITY FOR YOUR ACTIONS EMPOWERS YOU

OK, so at this point you can see there is a resiliency advantage that accrues from decisive action. The next step is to take responsibility for your actions.

Martin Seligman has argued that as a society, we have protected our children from the pain of disappointment by convincing them that they're not responsible for their actions. In doing so we appear to have created an epidemic of young adults who have been deprived of one of life's great teachers—taking responsibility for one's failure. The English philosopher Herbert Spencer once noted, "The ultimate result of shielding men from the effects of folly is to fill the world with fools." Only by taking responsibility for our failures do we benefit from the empowerment of taking credit for our subsequent successes.

Taking personal responsibility requires courage, perhaps more courage than being decisive. After all, most of us believe that mistakes are who we are, rather than what we did. We're quick to seek other people or things to blame should the outcome of a decision not be as desirable as hoped. In doing so, we abdicate responsibility for failure and forfeit the potential benefit to be gained from rebirth. Only by taking responsibility for our actions can we then learn to take credit for our successes. This fuels the halo effect and, subsequently, the self-fulfilling prophecy. We become the beneficiary of all those empowering predictors of success simply by learning to take responsibility for our actions.

One of the most resilient men during the American Civil War was Confederate General Robert E. Lee. He was a man who accepted responsibility for his actions.

In July 1863, in an attempt to end the war, Lee took the Army of Northern Virginia into Maryland, ostensibly as a demonstration of the vulnerability of the North. The Union Army of the Potomac engaged Lee's army at Gettysburg, Pennsylvania. The battle lasted three days, with Lee winning the first day, and Union forces, under the command of General George Meade, winning the second day.

In an effort to win the battle and perhaps the war, Lee ordered a risky, if not seemingly suicidal, charge against Union positions on an area known as Cemetery Ridge.

Lee's most trusted generals vehemently disagreed with the plan of attack and tried to convince him it would be a disaster. Indeed, the attack on Cemetery Ridge, called Pickett's Charge, emerged as a horrific failure. Some say it was the day the Confederacy lost the Civil War. It was reported that as Confederate forces were in retreat, a demoralized Confederate General Wilcox approached General Lee and described the failure of his brigade. Lee interrupted him, shook his hand, and said, "Never mind, General, all this is my fault—it is I that have lost this fight, and you must help me out of it the best way you can."

In the 1998 book *The Words Lincoln Lived By*, author Gene Griessman describes another brilliantly resilient man of the same era and same conflict: Abraham Lincoln. According to Griessman, Lincoln accepted the blame for the Union failures early in the Civil War. In an amazing gesture, after the Battle of Gettysburg, when the fate of the Union appeared to change, Lincoln sent this message to General Meade:

> You will follow up and attack General Lee as soon as possible before he can cross the river. If you fail this dispatch will clear you from all responsibility, and if you succeed, you may destroy it.

Taking responsibility for your own actions aids in gaining empowerment. The "halo" derived from decisiveness and self-responsibility will generalize to other aspects of your personal and professional lives. Winston Churchill considered Lee one of the greatest generals in the history of Western civilization. And presidential historians consider Lincoln the greatest American president of all time.

Your resiliency advantage accrues not only from the fruits of opportunities pursued and the empowerment of success in the wake of adversity, but from the fact that many people will view your decisiveness before, during, or after adversity as evidence of courage, strength, and desirability that extends to your entire persona. Taking responsibility for your actions will be interpreted as evidence of honesty and trustworthiness. Consequently, you'll often be given opportunities that others will be denied. And since your failures will be seen as uncharacteristic exceptions to the rule, you'll likely be given greater leniency in the wake of failure and more chances to succeed.

Michael Jordan (born February 17, 1963), according to the National Basketball Association (NBA) website, has been acclaimed as the greatest basketball player of all time. He is also the owner of the Charlotte Bobcats basketball team.

After leading the University of North Carolina Tar Heels to the 1982 NCAA National Championship, he was drafted by the Chicago Bulls of the NBA. In 1991, 1992, and 1993, he led the Bulls to the NBA Championship. In a move that shocked the sporting world and made international headlines, Jordan announced his retirement from basketball on October 6, 1993. He said he had lost the desire to play basketball. Jordan's motivation to play the game he had previously loved and dominated seemed to all but vanish when, in July 1993, his father was murdered by two teenagers on the side of a highway.

In what seemed to be an attempt to honor his father, Jordan signed a contract to play minor league baseball. His father had believed Jordan would be a professional baseball player when Michael was younger. His baseball career was short-lived, however. Jordan returned to professional basketball and led the Bulls to NBA Championships in 1996, 1997, and 1998.

Jordan's successes are what most people remember. What they forget are his failures that ultimately led to his remarkable series of successes. Not only did Jordan rebound from the devastating loss of his father, but he rebounded from all manner of failure. Jordan once said, "I can accept failure, everyone fails at something. But I can't accept not trying." Before his career finally ended with six NBA Championships, Jordan was voted NBA Most Valuable Player five times. In 1999, ESPN named him the greatest North American athlete of the 20th century.

SEVEN BARRIERS TO DECISIVENESS AND
TAKING RESPONSIBILITY

No doubt there are many barriers to decisive action and accepting personal responsibility. Look at the list below and put a check next to the items that seem most applicable to you.

- ❐ 1. Paralyzing fear of failure
- ❐ 2. Fear of ridicule
- ❐ 3. Procrastination; waiting too long to act
- ❐ 4. Failure to succinctly communicate relevant details concerning your actions, leading to confusion and hesitation to act
- ❐ 5. Trying to please everyone; involving too many people in the decision-making process

❐ 6. Being overwhelmed by the scope of the challenge (or with data) and consequently losing the ability to quickly and effectively distinguish between highly relevant and marginally relevant information in the decision-making process

❐ 7. Losing sight of the long-term goal while enacting emotionally driven, feel-good, palliative solutions; relieving the pain without dealing with the underlying cause

The first step in reaching a solution is recognition of the problem. How many of the seven barriers to decisiveness and self-responsibility did you check off? Ask yourself what the origins of such inclinations might have been. Then ask yourself, "How are they working out?" The most common answer is that they work well as long as safety and mediocrity are your goals. But if those were your goals, you probably would not be reading this book.

RX: PRESCRIPTIONS FOR INCREASING DECISIVENESS AND TAKING PERSONAL RESPONSIBILITY

Let's look at some solutions for each of the problems enumerated above.

1. Problem: Paralyzing fear of failure

Solution: Never forget this simple guiding principle: Anything worth having is worth failing for. And don't forget the words of Friedrich Nietzsche: "What does not kill me makes me stronger."

We mentioned Al Neuharth in Chapter One. Neuharth, creator of the pioneering newspaper *USA Today*, once said, "Everyone should fail in a big way at least once before they're forty. The bigger you fail, the bigger you're likely to succeed later."

In 1952, Neuharth and his friend Bill Porter raised $50,000 to launch *SoDak Sports*, a weekly newspaper in South Dakota. The publication failed in two years, due, in Neuharth's opinion, to his own mismanagement. At age 30, he was hired as a reporter for the *Miami Herald*. He advanced within the *Herald*'s parent company, the Knight newspaper organization, until Gannett hired him. He built Gannett into the largest newspaper company in the United States. Then, in 1982, he founded *USA Today,* the third most widely read newspaper in the country as of 2013.

"Failure shouldn't stop your drive to succeed," Neuharth once said. "How you respond to failure makes all the difference." He claimed that his success at *USA Today* would never have been possible without his failure in South Dakota.

So go out there and fail at least once in a big way.

2. Problem: Fear of ridicule for being different. It's no fun to be laughed at.

Solution: Most people ridicule what they do not understand. In his 2008 bestselling book *Outliers*, author Malcolm Gladwell makes a cogent argument that extraordinary success is often predicated upon being different. Gladwell describes people who were not only different but possessed what many thought of as liabilities.

Take the case of attention deficit hyperactivity disorder (ADHD), a neurologically based disorder in which one has great difficulty maintaining sustained attention. One's mind wanders, but the biggest problem is the enhanced distractibility. People with ADHD often have problems in traditional academic settings. They get poor grades and often leave formal schooling prematurely. Interestingly, they often possess attributes that others lack, such as creativity, compassion, drive, an aptitude for quick and effective problem solving, the ability to see the forest when others are stuck in the trees, and perhaps even intuition.

If this describes you, don't give up on your dreams despite the hardship and even the ridicule. Instead, find advisers and mentors who appreciate your differences, and when conformity is a problem, remember the Miley Cyrus Effect: What does not kill my career makes it stronger.

3. Problem: Procrastination. Waiting too long to act. The desire to wait until the moment of absolute certainty before making a decision can be compelling. To begin, it's hard to overcome inertia. Add the risk of making a mistake, and we easily see that decisive action can be difficult to achieve.

Solution: What we too often fail to understand is that almost all opportunities come with time limits. As we wait for that moment of absolute certainty, we also see the window of opportunity become smaller, until the opportunity is lost. In the words of Mark Twain, "I was seldom able to see an opportunity until it had ceased to be one."

If you are procrastinating because a task seems overwhelming, simply use the "Swiss cheese" technique. This is a method recommended by time management expert Alan Lakein in his book *How to Get Control of Your Time and Your Life*. Rather than avoiding something because it seems overwhelming, break it into smaller, more manageable component tasks and do one of the more manageable tasks at a time. Eventually, by doing one component task at a time, you will have completed the entire project. Setting goals with achievable milestones and using approaches like the "Swiss cheese" technique can be a very effective way of approaching an otherwise overwhelming task.

4. Problem: Failure to succinctly communicate details concerning your intentions or actions may lead to confusion and hesitation to act.

Solution: Use the resilient moment communications model. When communicating to others regarding the necessity for change or the emergence of a problem requiring attention, adhere to the following formula:

- Describe the *need* to act or change in some way. This may be a personnel problem, a change in market conditions, a change in resources, or an unanticipated crisis.
- Describe the *cause* of the problem.
- Describe the *effects* of the problem. These effects may be those already realized and/or those anticipated.
- Describe specifically what *action* will be taken.
- Describe, if relevant, what actions may be taken so as to reduce the likelihood of a recurrence of the problem, if not already indicated.

5. Problem: Involving too many people in the decision-making process in an attempt to please everyone, or in an attempt to attain perfection, while disregarding the attainment of excellence.

Solution: Research in managerial styles seems to indicate that when you desire a creative solution without the pressure of time urgency, larger decision-making groups can be highly effective. However, if you find yourself on the verge of the abyss with little time, a smaller decision-making group may be more effective. Sometimes you will have to make the decision yourself.

6. Problem: Being overwhelmed by too much information, too wide a scope, or too little time.

Solution:

- *Remember the 80/20 Rule*: 80 percent of your problem comes from 20 percent of the potential sources. It's a derivation of the skewed (non-Bell–shaped) distribution of Power Law statistics. For example, 80 percent of all healthcare costs come in the last 20 percent of your life. Eighty percent, or more, of polluting vehicle emissions come from only 20 percent of all vehicles. Eighty percent of casualties in a terrorist attack will be psychological as opposed to physical. You get the point. So rather than view problems as being universal and paralyzing, search for the applicability of the 80/20 Rule. Focus on the minority of potential sources that may account for the majority of the problem. Then, if appropriate, apply your resources to the 20 percent. Malcolm Gladwell concludes that if you use this approach, you may actually be able to solve a problem rather than simply palliatively manage it.
- *Try practicing Occam's razor (a.k.a. the law of simplicity)*: When faced with competing alternative courses of action or competing conclusions, choose the one that rests upon the fewest assumptions.

Also, to further simplify, understand the nature of the problem you face. Is it a puzzle or is it a mystery?

Malcolm Gladwell argues that puzzles represent questions that have known answers. Puzzles require a finite amount of information. All you have to do is discover a sufficient number of pieces to the puzzle in order to solve it.

Mysteries, on the other hand, represent questions that do not have currently existing answers. In order to solve a mystery, discovery is insufficient. Rather, you must make judgments regarding uncertainty. You must anticipate and prognosticate. All of this is done based on assumptions.

Finding Osama bin Laden was a puzzle. Predicting what the stock market will do is a mystery. Gladwell argues that the biggest mistake you can make is to assume that a mystery (e.g., predicting future behavior) is a puzzle. That assumption will lead you to a never-ending search for the "facts" that will solve the mystery, when in reality those facts might not currently exist. Gladwell concludes that in your quest to solve the mystery, you can obtain so much information that it paralyzes your ability to act or leads you in the wrong direction.

Predicting the future of the stock market using descriptive and inferential statistics is called *technical analysis*. The problem with technical analysis is that it assumes current stock market data will predict future moves in the market. In other words, it assumes that predicting the future of the stock market is a puzzle that can be solved by analyzing price trends, stochastics, volume, and other putatively predictive indicators. But predicting what the stock market will do is not a puzzle. It's a mystery. Technical analysis catastrophically failed to predict the depth or duration of the stock market crash of 2007–2008.

7. Problem: Taking your eye off of the ball. Losing sight of the goal while enacting the least disruptive and emotionally driven, feel-good palliative solutions.

Solution: Apply this variation of Pascal's wager, sometimes referred to as the best-case/worst-case analysis. When faced with a challenging decision, ask yourself these questions:

- What's the best thing that's likely to happen if I act?
- What's the worst thing that's likely to happen if I act?
- What's the best thing that's likely to happen if I do not act?
- What's the worst thing that's likely to happen if I do not act?

Then make your choice.

HOMEWORK

Pick one thing you can do, starting next Monday, that will help you be decisive and increase personal responsibility. Write it here:

_____

_____

_____

Now send yourself an email as a reminder.

CHAPTER 3

THE MORAL COMPASS: HONESTY, INTEGRITY, FIDELITY, AND ETHICAL BEHAVIOR

In Chapter One we discussed the foundation of our version of resiliency, active optimism. In those who are truly resilient, optimism becomes a self-fulfilling prophecy. In Chapter Two we argued that optimism is not enough. In order to resiliently bounce back when life has knocked you down, you must be decisive and act. Nevertheless, we acknowledged decisive action was often very difficult in the wake of adversity.

Here in Chapter Three, we'll introduce a notion that may make difficult decisions easier. Here we argue that your ascent from the darkness of the abyss is made easier when you use the guiding light of the moral compass. But before we dive in, it's time for another self-assessment.

SELF-ASSESSMENT #3

Directions: Circle the answer that best describes how strongly you agree with the following statements.

1. *It's important to tell the truth.*

    1—Strongly disagree

    2—Disagree

    3—Agree

    4—Strongly agree

2. *Withholding information (telling a half-truth) is dishonest.*

    1—Strongly disagree

    2—Disagree

    3—Agree

    4—Strongly agree

3. *It is important to act in a consistent and reliable manner.*

    1—Strongly disagree

    2—Disagree

    3—Agree

    4—Strongly agree

4. *Loyalty should seldom depend upon the situation.*

    1—Strongly disagree

    2—Disagree

    3—Agree

    4—Strongly agree

5. *The needs of the many outweigh the needs of the few.*

    1—Strongly disagree

    2—Disagree

    3—Agree

    4—Strongly agree

This self-assessment is not a clinical diagnostic tool. It is simply a survey designed to motivate you to think about your attitudes concerning the moral compass. When you have completed the survey, add up the numbers next to the answers you have circled for items #1–5. The lowest score you can have is 5; the highest is 20.

Items #1 and #2 reflect the notion of honesty. Item #1, "It's important to tell the truth," reflects the unqualified degree of importance honesty holds for you. We assume that by endorsing this item with "Agree" or "Strongly agree," you would also endorse the notion that lying is undesirable.

Item #2, "Withholding information (telling a half-truth) is dishonest," complicates things a bit. This item examines what some may think of as acceptable, while others see it as just a veiled form of dishonesty. The answer may reside in the intention. From our perspective, if the intention is to deceive, then a half-truth is dishonest.

Item #3 looks at a form of integrity when it states: "It is important to act in a consistent and reliable manner." Integrity may be hard to recognize so we focus here on one of the most common manifestations of integrity: reliability. The most desirable form of reliability is an incorruptible pattern of honesty. In physics, structural integrity yields reliable performance under pressure. With regard to human behavior, reliability emerges from a foundation of structural integrity at the intrapsychic level. Some will ask, "What about those who are reliably dishonest?" While reliable dishonesty does not seem to help one be resilient, the recognition of reliable dishonesty in others can assist you in avoiding such people when you are in search of assistance.

Items #4 and 5 reflect ethical behavior. Ethical behavior is that behavior that supports the greater good. Although we are sure there will be rare exceptions, seldom is ethical behavior situation dependent. Similarly, ethical behavior reflects an acknowledgment that the needs for the greater good of a group as a whole should outweigh the needs of a few members of that group.

Now let's take a closer look at honesty, integrity, fidelity, and ethical conduct with regard to resiliency.

"I serve with honor. . . . Uncompromising integrity is my standard. My character and honor are steadfast. My word is my bond." This passage from the U.S. Navy SEAL Ethos summarizes in clear and concise terms the essence of virtuous resilience that follows a moral compass. Mark Twain simplified this concept in a 1901 speech to the Young People's Society at Brooklyn's Greenpoint Presbyterian Church: "Always do right. This will gratify some people, and astonish the rest." Twain later observed that physical courage seems common, but moral courage very rare.

THE FOUR POINTS OF THE MORAL COMPASS

We chose the notion of a compass to anchor our discussion because when you find yourself in the darkness of the abyss of despair, when the temptation is to bend the rules, use deception, take advantage of others, and even cheat, the compass will help you choose the right direction, make decisions you will not have to apologize for later, and ultimately find your way from the darkness of the abyss to the light of success. The term *moral compass* may be thought to denote any tool that serves to guide or direct your system of virtues (*virtue* is derived from the Greek meaning goodness, positive qualities).

In this chapter, we suggest that the moral compass for resilience consists of four points—honesty, integrity, fidelity, and ethical behavior—which collectively can help you navigate in the direction of virtue no matter how turbulent your journey in life may be. Although these terms are often used interchangeably, we believe there are important differences and that one builds upon the other.

Nevertheless, they are all qualities we admire in others, value in society, and, hopefully, strive for in ourselves. Why do we admire and reinforce these qualities? Why are they critical elements in the formation of the psychological body armor that fuels your resilience? And why do they bestow a resiliency advantage? Let's take a closer look.

FOLLOWING A MORAL COMPASS CREATES A RESILIENCY ADVANTAGE

We believe that the moral compass not only guides you to a virtuous life but also bestows a resiliency advantage that will assist you in times of adversity and provide you with an advantage over others in almost all aspects of life. Honesty, integrity, fidelity, and ethical behavior are all qualities we admire and value in society because they are qualities that contribute to social cohesion. Cohesive societies, like cohesive organizations, tend to function more effectively. These qualities support innovation and cooperation.

Finally, the four points of the moral compass are attributes that we value and actually search for in others.

Honesty, integrity, fidelity, and ethical behavior tend to remove the risk from business and personal relationships. They offer interpersonal predictability; predictability engenders safety; and safety fosters trustworthiness. When you deal in business or personal relationships, others will never have to worry who "has their back" because their back will never be in danger. An amazing thing happens when you are perceived as trustworthy: You will be given greater responsibility that will lead to more opportunities.

Now let's take a closer look at the four points of the moral compass: honesty, integrity, fidelity, and ethical behavior.

HONESTY

Honesty may be thought of as being truthful. Honesty may be thought of as being genuine. It is the absence of deception, fraud, or deliberate misrepresentation.

Dishonesty, on the other hand, is the presence of disingenuousness. If your intention is to deceive, so as to harm another, or to achieve personal gain or advantage, then that is dishonesty. Cheating (taking unfair advantage) is dishonest. Any advantage that is gained through dishonesty seems brittle and short-lived. Dishonesty is often born of urgency, impulsivity, and greed. For most people, dishonesty seems most associated with situational stress and a lack of personal resiliency. For this reason, so-called honesty tests are generally poor predictors of dishonesty.

The last 20 years in professional sports has been an era during which, some believe, cheating and dishonesty have abounded. The June 4, 2012, issue of *Sports Illustrated* ran a provocative article by

Tom Verducci titled "To Cheat or Not to Cheat." In it, Verducci chronicled how steroids affected the lives of aspiring professional baseball players seeking to gain a competitive advantage in their quest for the major leagues.

Then there's what ESPN refers to as "the steroids era." This was a period of time in US major league baseball when a number of already established players were believed to have used performance-enhancing drugs, resulting in record-setting offensive performances. From 2005 through 2013, 44 major-league baseball players were suspended for using banned performance-enhancing substances.

Then, perhaps most blatantly, there's the high-profile case of cyclist Lance Armstrong.

LANCE ARMSTRONG

The Tour de France, which originated in 1903, is one of the world's most prestigious athletic events. It may also be the most grueling. The race, consisting of 21 day-long segments over a 23-day period, covers approximately 2,000 miles in distance. While the route changes each year, it always involves passages through the Pyrenees and Alps, with the finish coming on the Champs-Élysées in Paris.

Lance Armstrong began professional cycling in 1992. In 1996, he was diagnosed with testicular cancer that had spread to his brain and lungs. Aggressive treatments resulted in Armstrong's being declared cancer free in 1997. He resumed his career in 1998 and, in doing so, became an icon for those with cancer. He later founded Livestrong, a charity that supports cancer patients and survivors.

In a feat that seemed superhuman, Armstrong competed in and won the Tour de France in 1999 and a record six more times in a row. In June 2012, the United States Anti-Doping Agency charged Armstrong with having used performance-enhancing drugs. That August, it banned Armstrong from competition for life. In January 2013, Armstrong went on the *Oprah Winfrey Show* and responded to five yes/no questions Winfrey posed:

1. Did Armstrong take banned substances? "Yes."
2. Was one of those EPO (erythropoietin)? "Yes."
3. Did he do blood doping and use transfusions? "Yes."
4. Did he use testosterone, cortisone, and human growth hormone? "Yes."
5. Did he take banned substances or blood dope in all his Tour wins? "Yes."

Armstrong seemed to justify his actions by indicating that he did not think he was cheating but simply creating a level playing field. According to ESPN in 2013, "Lance Armstrong acknowledges he hasn't been the nicest guy in the world, but he says if he had to do it over again, he would still dope because everyone else in cycling was doping too."

"I knew what my competitors were doing. We [his U.S. Postal Service team] were doing less," Armstrong said in an interview for *ESPN The Magazine*. "We were more conservative, and that's the reason we were never going to be caught.

"This is a story because I was a bigger a—h———. Because I was more litigious. Because I was more combative.

... And I've heard from a lot of people who say, 'You made all the money, you got all the fame, you deserve this.' And I hear that, and I understand that people think that way. . . ."

Armstrong felt that he was singled out and ultimately stripped of his record seven Tour de France titles because he fought back so hard against those who accused him of doping.

What do you think? If you find yourself in a situation where everyone else is breaking the rules, is it really cheating for you to break the rules as well? Assume for a moment that Armstrong's implication that other cyclists were using performance-enhancing drugs is correct. If so, did his use of those drugs constitute cheating? Similarly, given the plethora of baseball players using performance-enhancing drugs, were they really cheating?

For an answer, let's look at professional golfer Brian Davis.

Like baseball, golf is also a game of numerous rules. But most important, golf is a game of self-enforced honesty. Rule 13.4, for example, calls for a two-stroke penalty if your golf club moves any loose impediment during your backswing. On April 18, 2010, while playing in the first hole of a championship playoff at the Verizon Heritage Cup in Hilton Head, South Carolina, English golfer Brian Davis called Rule 13.4 on himself. While taking his backswing in an attempt to hit his ball out of a hazard, Davis believed that he had grazed a reed sticking out of the sand. He immediately asked the official if he had seen an infraction. The official did not. They then used high-speed cameras with slow-motion replay. The video replay analysis revealed that Davis had indeed touched the reed. Davis called a two-stroke penalty on himself and conceded the tournament to his opponent. While Davis's decision may have cost him a chance at his first PGA Tour win (and the $1.02 million first place prize), he probably won the respect of many who play the "royal and ancient game" of golf.

OK, so, now it's your turn. Let's make the discussion more personal.

List one example of a situation where someone (including yourself) in your personal or professional life did something that showed a lack of honesty:

_____

_____

_____

Now list one example of someone (including yourself) in your personal or professional life who did something that showed honesty in a difficult or challenging situation:

_____

_____

_____

Before we leave this section on honesty, please reflect on the following:

You are interviewing a 23-year-old job candidate. As part of the security assessment, you ask about any previous problems with the legal system. Specifically, you ask if the candidate has ever been arrested. He replies, "No."

Finding his credentials acceptable, you offer him employment. Three months later, the new employee is performing well above expected levels. He seems happy with the job, he performs well with co-workers, and you are pleased to have him as an employee. He seems to have significant advancement potential.

As part of the employment screening process, you had sent out brief questionnaires to his neighbors. One of the neighbors, who had misplaced the form and thus delayed sending it back, indicated that the employee had been arrested when he was younger. You call the employee in to discuss the matter. In that discussion, he reveals that he was arrested for shoplifting as part of a fraternity prank when he 21 years old, but that his record had been expunged. His attorney explained to him that his case records had been sealed, to the effect that in the eyes of the law, he had never been arrested.

He seems very sincere in his understanding of the events. When you asked him why he did not simply reveal the incident, he replied he was sure he would not get the job if he did, but more important, he said he relied on his attorney's statement that in the eyes of the law, the arrest had never occurred.

So, what do you think about the following?

- Do you think the employee was dishonest in his interview?
- Should he be fired for not disclosing the incident?
- If he is retained, should any disciplinary action be taken?
- Has this eroded your trust in him? Could you trust him in the future?

INTEGRITY

Now let's turn to the second point on the moral compass, integrity. While integrity is sometimes defined as honesty, we actually see it as virtuous reliability and consistency that is built on a foundation of honesty. Integrity may be thought of as reliable incorruptibility and uncompromising sincerity.

The word *integrity* is derived from the Greek word *integra*, which means whole. In his treatise *The German Mind: A Philosophical Diagnosis*, the philosopher George Santayana stated, "Our character . . . is an omen of our destiny, and the more integrity we have and keep, the simpler and nobler that destiny is likely to be." Consistent with Santayana's view, integrity may be seen as a character of incorruptibility.

In a CNBC posting on July 9, 2013, Holly Ellyatt reported on the largest global survey on corruption ever conducted. That year, Transparency International surveyed more than 114,000 respondents in more than 100 countries. The survey revealed 55 percent of respondents indicating special interest groups unduly influenced government. According to the report, "Around the world, political parties, the driving force of democracies, are perceived to be the most corrupt institution."

Warren Buffet is one of the world's richest men, having built, from relatively meager beginnings, an international investment empire. He is, for many, a paragon of business success. On the issue of integrity, he offers a personal imperative, as well as an organizational admonition: "It takes 20 years to build a reputation and five minutes to ruin it. If you think about that, you'll do things differently." From the organizational perspective, he notes, "In looking for people to hire, you look for three qualities: integrity, intelligence, and energy. And if they don't have the first, the other two will kill you."

During the week of May 19, 2014, Fox News TV anchor Neil Cavuto closed a segment with a comment on success. He noted that students often approach him and inquire about the key to success. He said they are almost always disappointed in his answer. He tells them the key to being successful is to be reliable. Show up on time, do what you say you are going to do, and remember, promises don't have expiration dates.

OK, now it's your turn, again:

List one example of someone (including yourself) in your personal or professional life exhibiting a lack of integrity:

_____

_____

_____

Now list one example of someone (including yourself) in your personal or professional life demonstrating a high degree of integrity in a difficult or challenging situation:

_____

_____

_____

FIDELITY

Our third point on the moral compass is fidelity, which means faithfulness and dedication. The Latin phrase *semper fidelis*—adopted by the U.S. Marine Corps as its motto in 1883—means always faithful. The concept of fidelity as a core attribute dates back at least 200 years earlier in England, where it was a motto for aristocratic families and even entire cities.

Fidelity is a precious commodity. American history reveals just how through the remarkable life of General Benedict Arnold. In his 1990 biography of Arnold, *Patriot and Traitor*, author Willard S. Randall discusses the fragility of fidelity.

Many historians consider the Battles of Saratoga to be the turning point in the American Revolutionary War. During the fall of that year, in a bold strategic advance, British General John Burgoyne set out in a campaign to divide New England from the southern colonies. By dividing the colonies, the British hoped to isolate the colonial armies and eventually win a war of attrition.

Burgoyne was encouraged by winning a small victory over General Horatio Gates in the September 19 battle at Saratoga, but he sustained significant losses. On October 7, he again attacked the American forces. Due to the bravery and tactical vision of American General Benedict Arnold, the British forces were defeated. Finding that his army had been surrounded by the much larger American force, Burgoyne was compelled to surrender on October 17.

The Battles of Saratoga were deemed the most significant of the war, and Arnold's leadership the most compelling, because Burgoyne's surrender was the key factor that convinced the French to enter the war in support of the Americans. During the battle, Arnold's horse was shot out from under him, falling on his leg. This incident proved crippling to Arnold. While General George Washington recognized the efforts and bravery of Arnold, the Continental Congress was loath to do so because of a series of altercations that had spanned several years. Arnold was known to have a "quick temper." These events created an environment of mutual disrespect and mistrust.

Following the Battles of Saratoga and the withdrawal of British forces, General Washington gave Arnold command of the city of Philadelphia. There he met and married Peggy Shippen, whom many had believed was a British sympathizer. In 1779, fueled by his hatred of the Continental Congress, which he believed conspired to persecute him, Arnold began negotiations with the British, in the person of Shippen's former friend and confidant, the British Major John Andre. Arnold would agree to surrender the fort at West Point, New York, which he came to command, in exchange for a considerable amount of money and appointment as an officer in the British army.

His treason was discovered when Andre was captured. Arnold fled to London with his wife. Andre was hanged as a spy. Despite the pleadings of British and American military personnel to spare Andre's life, George Washington refused. He even denied numerous requests to have Andre shot by a firing squad, rather than be hanged (hanging was deemed the lowest form of execution possible for a military officer). As for Arnold, though he was rewarded for his service to the British, it was said they never really trusted him. Arnold died in England in 1801. His wife died four years later.

Despite his bravery and contribution to the ultimate defeat of the British in the Revolutionary War, there are no explicit monuments to Benedict Arnold. His name is associated with treachery and betrayal. George Washington reportedly forbade that Arnold's name be memorialized. Interestingly, the so-called Boot Monument—a Revolutionary War memorial in Saratoga National Historical Park that bears the likeness of a military boot—commemorates Benedict Arnold's heroic actions at the Battles of Saratoga without naming him. As mentioned earlier, Arnold sustained a crippling leg injury when his horse was shot out from under him. The dedication on the Boot Monument reads, "Erected 1887 By John Watts de Peyster. In memory of the 'most brilliant soldier' of the Continental Army who was desperately wounded on this spot . . . 7th October, 1777 winning for his countrymen the decisive battle of the American Revolution and for himself the rank of Major General." Thus, so egregious was Arnold's betrayal, only his boot was memorialized in a positive manner.

Let's fast forward to May 2013. Edward Snowden, an American computer specialist employed as a Booz Allen Hamilton contractor at the National Security Agency (NSA), has leaked top-secret papers to the British newspaper the *Guardian*. Snowden's leaks detailed telephone- and Internet-surveillance programs conducted by the U.S. and British governments.

These surveillance programs are seen by some as a violation of an individual's right to privacy, but others argue the programs were appropriately sanctioned and necessary for national security. A report in the *Wall Street Journal* claimed the NSA's surveillance network had the capacity to monitor approximately 75 percent of all U.S. Internet communications.

According to numerous sources in the intelligence community, Snowden's leaks have proven significantly harmful, jeopardizing intelligence resources and causing potential enemies of the United States to change their patterns of communications. On June 14, 2013, federal prosecutors charged Snowden with espionage and theft. Prior to the leaks being made public, Snowden had left the United States for Hong Kong, ultimately being granted temporary asylum in Russia.

Snowden's actions have created a firestorm of controversy. The granting of asylum served to strain U.S. and Russian relations. Some call Snowden a narcissistic traitor, while others see him as a whistle-blowing patriot. Even former U.S. President Jimmy Carter seemed to lend support to Snowden's actions, according to some press reports.

Snowden responded to his critics by saying his actions were designed to inform the public of what their governments were doing. In a statement he made from a Moscow airport, he cited the principles declared at the 1945 post–World War II Nuremberg proceedings: "Individuals have international duties which transcend the national obligations of obedience. Therefore individual citizens have the duty to violate domestic laws to prevent crimes against peace and humanity from occurring."

So what do you think? Did Edward Snowden act with fidelity? If so, to whom and why? If not, why not? Is Snowden a patriot or a traitor? Why?

U.S. NAVY SEALS GLEN DOHERTY AND TYRONE WOODS

While the debate surrounding Snowden's fidelity may never be resolved, other recent events give us a far clearer picture of what courage and fidelity look like. Two former U.S. Navy SEALs, Glen Doherty and Tyrone Woods, who died defending the U.S. Consulate in Benghazi, Libya, in 2012, have been nominated to posthumously receive the Congressional Gold Medal. Their courage and dedication seem a fitting example in this section on fidelity.

Benghazi is a port city on the Mediterranean Sea. It is the second-largest city in Libya, after the capital, Tripoli. On September 11, 2012, the American diplomatic mission compound at Benghazi sustained a well-planned attack by heavily armed anti-American forces. Reports indicate the attack began around 9:40 p.m. and was directed at the diplomatic compound where Ambassador Chris Stevens was at the time.

Former Navy SEAL Tyrone Woods was part of a small security team, including Mark Geist, Kris Paronto, and John Tiegen, that was housed at the CIA annex about one mile from the diplomatic compound. Woods and others requested permission to aid Ambassador Stevens and others in the compound. Fox News originally reported on Oct 26, 2012, that Woods was ordered to "stand down." This claim was denied by the State Department at the time. Nevertheless, issuance of the stand down order was later supported by Michael Zuckoff in his book *13 Hours: The Inside Account of What Really Happened in Benghazi*, based on in-depth interviews with the surviving CIA annex team members.

In September 2014, State Department spokeswoman Marie Harf denied that the security team was told to stand down but did say team members were told to delay for a short period. Despite apparent orders to the contrary, and at the risk of personal harm to themselves, Woods and the others left the annex to assist those in the compound. They later returned to the annex after retrieving the body of Sean Smith and some survivors from the compound.

At the annex, Woods was later joined by another retired Navy SEAL, Glen Doherty, and a team of other security personnel who had self-deployed from Tripoli by commandeering a private jet. Doherty and team members arrived around 5 a.m. September 12 after being held up at the airport for a few hours by Libyan officials. Shortly after arriving, the annex came under fire. Both Ty Woods and Glen Doherty were killed by mortar shells while taking up positions on the roof of the annex trying to defend the remaining U.S. personnel.

Craig Gustafson, writing for the *San Diego Union-Tribune* in May 2013, quoted SEAL Capt. Jason Ehret as saying, "Glen and Ty were the kind of men this country is proud to produce as citizens and as warriors. . . . That fateful night in Benghazi, they did what I expect any SEAL would have done. . . . They ran to the sound of gunfire. They had experienced all too well the hell of war and knew that Americans were in need of assistance. . . . We should all look to live like them."

Fidelity and dedication to duty are not the sole domain of Navy SEALs. Tom Brokaw, in his best-selling book *The Greatest Generation*, introduces us to this amazing generation by saying:

In the spring of 1984, I went to the northwest of France, to Normandy, to prepare an NBC documentary on the fortieth anniversary of D-Day. . . . There, I underwent a life-changing experience. As I walked the beaches with the American veterans who had returned for this anniversary . . . I was deeply moved and profoundly grateful for all they had done. Ten years later, I returned to Normandy for the fiftieth anniversary of the invasion, and by then I had come to understand what this generation of Americans meant to history. It is, I believe, the greatest generation any society has ever produced.

Quentin Aanenson and George S. Everly Sr. are members of that generation who displayed fidelity and sense of duty.

QUENTIN C. AANENSON

Quentin C. Aanenson (April 21, 1921–December 28, 2008) was a fighter pilot in the U.S. Army Air Corps. He served as a captain in the 391st Squadron, 9th Air Force. Aanenson served from 1942 to 1945. He flew the P-47 Thunderbolt during the Normandy invasion and campaign.

He told us the chances of survival were about 20 percent. He mentioned that one of the hardest aspects of his war experience was losing so many of his friends. He became so demoralized by the continual loss of his tent mates that he finally asked to live alone. His attitudes about war and, more important, about fidelity and dedication to duty are perhaps best captured in one of his letters to his wife, Jackie.

Dear Jackie,

For the past two hours, I've been sitting here alone in my tent, trying to figure out just what I should do and what I should say in this letter in response to your letters and some questions you have asked. I have purposely not told you much about my world over here, because I thought it might upset you. Perhaps that has been a mistake, so let me correct that right now. I still doubt if you will be able to comprehend it. I don't think anyone can who has not been through it.

I live in a world of death. I have watched my friends die in a variety of violent ways. . . . Sometimes it's just an engine failure on takeoff resulting in a violent explosion. There's not enough left to bury. Other times, it's the deadly flak that tears into a plane. If the pilot is lucky, the flak kills him. But usually he isn't, and he burns to death as his plane spins in. . . . You can't imagine the horror.

So far, I have done my duty in this war. I have never aborted a mission or failed to dive on a target no matter how intense the flak. I have lived for my dreams for the future. But like everything else around me, my dreams are dying, too. In spite of everything, I may live through this war and return to Baton Rouge. But I am not the same person you said goodbye to on May 3. No one can go through this and not change. We are all casualties. In the meantime, we just go on. Some way, somehow, this will all have an ending. Whatever it is, I am ready for it.

When we asked him what the saddest part of the war was for him, he said it was watching his wingman be shot down.

"We were flying so close our wings were overlapping. I saw he was hit. He went into a dive. I dove with him. He struggled to release his shoulder straps. Then in a moment he stopped. He was too low to bail out. He knew he was dead. He looked at me, smiled, waved, then crashed into the ground. What bothered me the most was I realized I saw the end of a generation. He was the last male in his family."

Fidelity and duty were important to Jackie as well. When asked how she able to hold up while Quentin was at war, she simply replied, in a wonderful Southern accent, "My job was to support my man! So that's what I did!"

The painting *Thunderbolt Patriot* by William R. Farrell at the National Air and Space Museum in Washington, DC, depicts Aanenson returning from a mission over Germany. An airfield in Luverne, Minnesota, his birthplace, was named after him: Quentin Aanenson Field Airport.

GEORGE S. EVERLY SR.

The family of George Everly Sr. (December 1, 1916–October 25, 2011) came to America in the late 1600s, settled in one locale, and farmed the land for 300 years. Growing up on a farm with no running water and no electricity, Everly did his schoolwork by lantern light.

Farming, however, was not to be his calling. He was the first male in his branch of the family to go to college. In fact, he was the first male in his direct line to be fully literate. Gifted in music, he turned professional musician at age 12 during the dawn of the Big Band Era. He was also a writer who became a correspondent for the top musical trade journal of the time, *Down Beat Magazine*.

To satisfy his service obligation, Everly enlisted into the U.S. Army. Soon, America went to war in World War II. He served in Iceland, England, France, Belgium, and Germany, where he saw destruction and death. He barely survived a missile attack when a German V-2 rocket fell onto a French farmhouse where he had established his radio communications. Some of his friends did not survive that attack.

He later survived the Battle of the Bulge, ultimately returning to America to marry Kathleen Webster, the woman he had met while stationed at Fort Benning, Georgia. Once home, Everly pursued a career—not in music, but in finance. He told us that although music was his great love, a full-time music career was not conducive to raising a family.

As was the tradition of the time, one's military service was a frequent topic of family discussions. The query, "What did you do in the war, Daddy?" was responded to by stories not of death and destruction, but of duty, camaraderie, and even travel. He said he was able to avoid the emotional trauma of war by staying mission focused and by always looking forward, rather than back. He said he never dwelled on negatives. He added that his religious faith helped him get through the war.

Fifty years later, when the French government offered D-Day campaign medals to Americans in 1994, Everly at first declined, then reluctantly accepted his medal seven years later, saying it just didn't seem all that important. This might not make sense to a subsequent generation that was raised expecting trophies simply for showing up.

Everly and his wife had one child. Life was relatively unremarkable for years as they lived the American middle-class dream. All of that would change because Kathleen suffered from a chronic illness. It would slowly rob her of her vivaciousness, her happiness, her ability to function independently, and eventually her life. During this period, Everly's financial career was progressing. Nevertheless, as his wife's illness worsened, Everly decided to forgo 24-hour nursing assistance and care for her himself as much as possible. Finally, the big day came in his career when he was offered the position of chief financial officer of his organization, a position he had worked 30 years to attain. He declined, deciding instead to retire in order to be better able to care for his wife.

During his life, Everly endured many challenges: farm life during the Great Depression, the trauma of war, and the stress of personally caring for his wife with a chronic debilitating illness after prematurely ending his career to do so. What are the lessons we can learn from this member of Brokaw's "greatest generation"?

- *Reliability*. Everly never missed a day of work. If he made a promise, he kept it.
- *Duty*. Everly understood that obligations to others often come before personal gratification or comfort.
- *Interpersonal support*. "Your relationships with other people are important," he said. "It is important to respect other people."
- *Optimism*. There is little value in looking back. He said, "Why waste time being upset?" About death, he said, "The future is a mystery regarding the afterlife. I'm curious." And then he added, "I think there's always something better in the future."

At his retirement and years later at his funeral, Everly was lauded simply. It was said of him, "He was a good man." Perhaps that was his and his generation's secret of resilience. Perhaps what made them "great" was that they were good people. They put a person on the moon, cured many diseases, and took steps to remedy many of the social ills that plagued their society and their nation. They would not be deterred. To reiterate the words of Brokaw, "It is, I believe, the greatest generation any society has ever produced." We agree.

Now let's do the exercise again.

List one example of someone (including yourself) in your personal or professional life exhibiting a lack of fidelity:

Now list one example of someone (including yourself) in your personal or professional life demonstrating a high degree of fidelity in a difficult or challenging situation:

ETHICAL BEHAVIOR

We began this chapter with honesty—a platform of truthfulness and absence of deception upon which we build a pattern of virtuous consistency and fidelity. Now we add the most complicated aspect of our moral compass: ethical behavior.

Ethics often refers to a code of conduct that is pro-social. Simply said, ethical behavior supports and enhances a society and serves the greater good. Ethics is often linked to morality. Ethical behavior may be thought of as acting harmoniously within prescribed values of fairness, as well as simply doing what is "right" and "just." Early philosophers such as Plato discussed ethical behavior, which seems essential to civilized society.

Ethical behavior, acting pro-socially, may be the most complex but important element in our moral compass; it serves as an action-oriented collective term for the other three points on the compass. Honesty, integrity, and fidelity must culminate in ethical behavior if they are to serve as psychological body armor. Mahatma Gandhi once said that there are seven things that will destroy society:

1. Wealth without work
2. Pleasure without conscience
3. Knowledge without character
4. Religion without sacrifice
5. Politics without principle
6. Science without humanity
7. Business without ethics

Sadly, examples of business without pro-social ethics are numerous. See if you think the events described below are examples of questionably ethical behavior. But remember, there are two sides to every story.

BRITISH PETROLEUM DEEPWATER HORIZON

British Petroleum (BP), a multinational oil and gas company headquartered in London, is the fifth-largest company in the world, operating in 80 countries. BP has extensive exploration, refinement, and distribution operations worldwide.

On April 20, 2010, an explosion occurred at 11 p.m. EST on the BP Deepwater Horizon oil rig in the Gulf of Mexico. As a result, 11 crew members were missing. On April 30, Tony Hayward, BP's CEO, told Reuters news service, "This is not our accident." Yet according to the Associated Press, "For days as the oil spill spread into the Gulf of Mexico . . . [Federal] authorities were content to let the company handle the mess." On May 1, President Barack Obama's administration named U.S. Coast Guard Adm. Thad Allen to direct the spill response. Progress seemed to accelerate.

Interestingly, in early May, the state of Alabama instructed BP to stop circulating settlement agreements to Alabama residents that would have voided their right to sue in exchange for a one-time payment of $5,000. About the same time, Hayward told NPR that BP is "fully responsible for cleanup and for 'legitimate' claims." He later told the BBC that BP was not responsible for the accident. "This was not our drilling rig, it was not our equipment, it was not our people."

According to a May 16, 2010, report on CBS's *60 Minutes*, the oil-drilling blowout preventer was damaged in a previously unreported accident four weeks before the April 20 explosion. BP declined to comment on the *60 Minutes* report. Calling into question the safety of oil drilling, a May 18 *Wall Street Journal* story said disaster plans for oil rigs are "lacking" and have been for many years. The article said that in 2004, BP managers warned in a trade journal "the company wasn't prepared for the long-term, round-the-clock task of dealing with a deep-sea spill."

However, on May 14, Hayward stated that the oil spill was "relatively minor" compared to the "very big ocean" (despite a NASA photo showing the oil spill to be about the size of Delaware). On June 1, Hayward declared, "We're sorry for the disruption. . . . There's no one who wants this over more than I do, I'd like my life back." BP denied the existence of underwater oil plumes, despite evidence to the contrary.

BP stock declined in value during this time. In August 2010, the leak was finally stopped, but not before Mr. Hayward was relieved of his position with BP. The *Associated*

Press reported on March 15, 2013, that BP asked a federal judge to block a court-appointed administrator from paying Gulf Coast businesses' claims through a multibillion-dollar settlement. Bloomberg reported that BP had asked U.S. District Judge Carl Barbier to stop some payments under the $8.5 billion oil-spill settlement, saying the administrator was misinterpreting damage claims, thus exposing the company to hundreds of millions of dollars' worth of fictitious losses. As cited in Bloomberg if Barbier refused that request, BP said it would ask him to ban payments on all economic-loss claims by any businesses in the industries in which BP claims the fictitious losses have been most prevalent.

Did BP act for the greater good? What do you think?

TYLENOL POISONINGS

Although often cited as an example of pro-social ethical corporate behavior, the case of the Tylenol poisonings bears repeating.

In Chicago, during September and October 1982, seven people died after taking Tylenol pain-relief capsules that had been laced with cyanide. Tylenol is made by Johnson & Johnson. At the time it was the company's best-selling product and the most popular pain reliever in the United States.

Almost immediately, Johnson & Johnson announced a massive product recall and free replacement program at an estimated cost of $100 million. The company also offered a $100,000 reward for the arrest of the person responsible for the poisoning. No arrests were ever made. The investigation revealed the poisoning to be limited in scope, so within a few months, Tylenol was once again offered for sale, but now with tamper-resistant packaging. Within a year, Tylenol sales had rebounded.

Even though the Tylenol poisonings occurred in 1982, it remains virtually iconic as a symbol of corporate integrity and ethical action in crisis. There can be little debate that Johnson & Johnson acted in a pro-social manner and did what was best for society, acting for the greater good.

Some ethicists argue that there is no universal right or wrong; ethical behavior, they say, is behavior that best serves society and supports the larger good. Ethical relativists would argue with regard to ethical behavior, "It just depends."

Are you an ethical relativist?

OK, one more time:

List one example of someone (including yourself) in your personal or professional life exhibiting a lack of ethical behavior:

Now list one example of someone (including yourself) in your personal or professional life demonstrating a high degree of ethical behavior in a difficult or challenging situation:

Last, pick one person whom you believe to personify all aspects of the moral compass of psychological body armor. And, most important, write a brief note explaining why you chose that person:

Why is the moral compass an important aspect of psychological body armor? When you see honesty, integrity, fidelity and ethical behavior in others, it creates a compelling atmosphere. They serve to create a role model for others. They immediately create a sense of predictability. Predictability creates a sense of safety. Safety inspires trust. For leaders of groups, organizations, societies, and even nations, trust creates compliance. Conversely, deception, duplicity, and dishonesty erode trust. They erode organizational, social, and even national effectiveness. People will be inclined to act to protect themselves and defend their actions, rather than thinking outside the norm and taking risks that could rapidly and significantly advance the group toward its goal.

THE MORAL COMPASS AT WORK

For C. A. "Dutch" Ruppersberger and Jonathan Adler, the moral compass matters. Both made courageous decisions because they felt that what they were doing was the right thing to do. Ruppersberger chose to pursue a career path that was personally and professionally risky. Adler chose to support a man unjustly accused and prosecuted.

CONGRESSMAN C. A. "DUTCH" RUPPERSBERGER

C. A. "Dutch" Ruppersberger (born January 31, 1946) is the current U.S. representative for Maryland's Second Congressional District. He was first elected to that position in 2003. Ruppersberger was the first Democratic freshman ever to be appointed to the House Permanent Select Committee on Intelligence. He is the ranking, or senior, member of the minority party on this committee most critical to sustaining national security.

Ruppersberger began his career as an assistant state's attorney in Baltimore County, Maryland. Promoted to chief of the investigative division, he vigorously pursued organized crime and political corruption. This was not always a popular course of action, nor was it without significant personal and professional risk.

While investigating a drug-trafficking case, Ruppersberger was involved in a near-fatal car accident. He credited his survival to the extraordinary care he received at the University of Maryland Shock Trauma Center. When Ruppersberger asked its founder, R. Adams Cowley, what he could do to repay the center that saved his life, Cowley suggested he run for office and fight for the funding necessary to save other victims of severe physical trauma. And so he did.

Initially defeated, he was eventually elected to the Baltimore County Council and later to the position of Baltimore County executive. Despite pressure to run for governor, Ruppersberger decided he could best serve his constituency by running for Congress and was elected to the House in

2002. He continues to support the Shock Trauma Center by serving on its oversight board of visitors.

Ruppersberger believes that one key to resiliency is attitude. "Get knocked down, get back up," he told us emphatically.

Ruppersberger's story of resilience didn't begin with his near-fatal accident. Born with asthma and a naturally competitive nature, he recalls struggling to overcome his physical limitations. He remembers visiting Ocean City, Maryland, each summer with his family. When he was 15, he saw a group of lifeguard candidates preparing to take the ocean swimming test. He asked if he, too, could take the test. Although he was wheezing with asthma, he wanted not just to complete the test but to beat the other candidates as well. Of course, he did, and was offered a summer job as a lifeguard on the Ocean City Beach Patrol—one of the youngest ever.

Later, he played through his asthma on the varsity football, swimming, and lacrosse teams at his high school and Baltimore City College. He also played college lacrosse at the perennial powerhouse of the University of Maryland and in international competition for Team USA in 1967. "I think asthma made me stronger," he concluded. "You make a decision to give in, or never give up."

For Ruppersberger, resiliency is about more than determination—it's about teamwork and integrity. Effective teams are based on honesty and loyalty, he said. A lesson he learned working on his family's farm, playing team sports, prosecuting criminals, and representing those who have put their faith in him as an elected official was, "You are only as good as your team." Ethical behavior is a cornerstone of who Ruppersberger is as a man. "I believe in the Golden Rule: Do unto others as you want them to do unto you," he said. "Just do the right thing, and everything else will take care of itself."

Ethical teamwork also means taking care of those in need. To veterans returning from war who are missing limbs or experiencing posttraumatic stress disorder, he said, "It's not enough to thank you for your service and sacrifice—we have an obligation to ensure you have the best possible quality of life. And you owe it to yourself to demand it."

According to Ruppersberger: "Life is precious and you should believe things will get better after you've been knocked down. I was close to paralyzed after my accident. Not only did I not give up, I wanted to recover faster than any of the doctors thought I could. Friendship and faith helped me. I believe in prayer, and it helped me to make it out of Shock Trauma."

"Congress is in bad shape right now because of partisan politics," Ruppersberger said. "The chairman of the House Intelligence Committee, Congressman Mike Rogers of Michigan, is a former FBI agent and I am a former prosecutor. As ranking member, or top Democrat, I like to tell him that all good FBI agents must listen to their prosecutors. But we roll up our sleeves and work together in a bipartisan way. At first, our committee was a snake pit because of the partisan groups. After time, the *Washington Post* wrote that things have changed. Congressman Rogers and I are getting things done. In fact, a major news network recently told us they wanted one of us—not both—for an interview on an intelligence matter because we agreed with each other too much."

Consider your legacy. Cooperation and mutual support helps everyone.

Make your legacy about integrity, Ruppersberger said. After all, you want to be respected for who you are and what you've done. "I want people to know that my motivation for what I am doing is to help people. Words are not enough. Never forget, actions define you, not your words."

JONATHAN H. ADLER

According to Jonathan Adler, "Victory is not defined by the receipt of a trophy, it's defined by the unrelenting honor in your heart." The corollary is that the title "honorable" is not bestowed upon those who hold a particular office. It's an adjective earned by deeds.

In 1991, Adler began his career in federal law enforcement as a revenue officer for the Internal Revenue Service. A revenue officer enforces collections for the IRS, pursuing individuals and businesses that are indebted to the federal government when that debtor is uncooperative or evasive. In our interview, Adler described this position as challenging. With no weapon or arrest authority, officers must nevertheless enforce financial penalties and seizures of property. Additionally, the job can be overwhelming, with the average caseload for each officer approximating 150 cases.

After completing three years as a field revenue officer, Adler said, he learned to handle daily adversity, be creative, and become better acquainted with the concept of honor. He ultimately became a criminal investigator, a position he holds today.

Adler's story of resiliency, however, does not relate to his role as a criminal investigator. Rather, it comes from his passion, his volunteer job. In 2008, Adler was elected national president of the Federal Law Enforcement Officers Association (FLEOA), the largest nonprofit, nonpartisan professional association representing active and retired federal law-enforcement officers. He is responsible for overseeing all aspects of FLEOA's mission and leading a membership of 26,000, representing 65 different federal agencies. His story involves honor, ethical behavior, and the courage to tenaciously do the right thing.

"A profound low point during my tenure as FLEOA national president was witnessing the inappropriate prosecution of an American hero who intervened in a case of domestic violence to save a battered woman's life" on Saint Thomas in the U.S. Virgin Islands, Adler told us.

According to CNN, on September 7, 2008, off-duty Special Agent Will Clark of the U.S. Bureau of Alcohol, Tobacco, Firearms and Explosives (ATF) witnessed his neighbors arguing in front of their housing complex. A large man, Marcus Sutkow, was threatening his girlfriend when Clark intervened in an attempt to de-escalate the hostilities. Clark's initial efforts failed. The 300-pound Sutkow smashed his girlfriend's vehicle with large stones and then shouted that he was going to his truck to get his gun to shoot her and Clark. He came out of his truck with a long steel flashlight, smashed Clark's car mirrors, and then charged him. Clark drew his weapon and shot Sutkow. He then kept Sutkow alive with CPR until emergency medical technicians arrived. Sutkow died at the hospital. Following the shooting Clark's gun and badge were taken as standard procedure for the duration of the investigation.

A multiple-agency federal investigation of the incident unanimously concluded the shooting was justified. The ATF returned Clark's gun and badge and returned him to duty. Nevertheless, Virgin Islands prosecutors charged Clark with second-degree murder. According to Adler:

"The subsequent investigation seemed terribly biased, as it excluded evidence supporting Will's claim of self-defense. Contrary to the spirit of our Constitution, Saint Thomas detectives discarded witness statements that corroborated Will's story. They failed to establish a crime scene and perform any forensic analysis. They failed to disclose the medical examiner's findings that the assailant was intoxicated at the time he was stopped. They quickly indicted Will for second-degree murder, portraying Will as some mainland thug.

"The judge ruled against Will on every motion and finally delivered the most defining commentary of this legal travesty. In response to Will's attorney filing a motion asserting immunity from island prosecution, and advocating Will's case be moved to federal court, the judge hollered, 'Your constitution doesn't follow you down here and doesn't apply.'

"I later challenged the chairman of the U.S. House Appropriations Subcommittee as to why our taxpayer dollars follow us down there, but our Constitution doesn't. He agreed to cut off the USVI, but it wasn't enough to stop the trial. Ultimately, the judge was removed. The charges against Will were ultimately dismissed after the government rested and failed to make their case.

"This incident was not only demoralizing for me, but it served to undermine everything I hold sacred as a law-enforcement professional and that for which I would give my life: the concept of justice. I had to bear daily witness to Will's mother as this miscarriage of justice unfolded. Fortunately, Will was cleared and able to travel home with his family with federal law-enforcement escorts.

"In spite of the fact that justice was ultimately served, this was probably the most disheartening experience in my FLEOA leadership role. I witnessed an honorable man unfairly prosecuted.

"Nevertheless, the FLEOA team never relented. There were some positive points and victories along the way, including having Will's agency pull all their assets out of the islands, in spite of the attorney general wanting them to remain. I believe we affected the decision to remove the first judge, which was critical to Will being cleared. And there were some lessons learned.

"While others perceived my leadership efforts as formidable, I didn't. Although I was proud of the relationship I developed with Will's mother and my advocacy for Will in Washington, I felt like I should have done more.

"I also witnessed the government for which I work and have sworn to uphold turn its back on an American hero. I came to understand it's not the enemy against whom you stand that matters; rather, it's for whom and for what you are fighting that really matters most.

"I learned to stay tenaciously true to my heart, to stay faithful to my ideals, and to continue to support the principles in which I believe, no matter how difficult that might be. Early on in the fight to defend Will, he emailed me a message that resonated with me deeply. He said he didn't worry about himself should he be convicted, but he didn't want his infant son to grow up without a father. I gave him my word that I wouldn't let that happen.

"When my advocacy failed to prevent Will from going to trial, I had the failure knot buried in my heart. Despite the repeated failures as we tried to support Will in his trial, I would not allow this story to end badly for him. We faced a judge and a law-enforcement system that seemed intent on condemning Will. At the same time we faced the apparent apathy of our own government and subtle messages to reduce our efforts in support of Will. But we would not quit.

"To all who will listen, I would suggest that your goals and priorities should not diminish due to a lack of progress. As long as there is an honorable goal to pursue, do so. Be flexible and adjust your pursuit as needed."

Fidelity is important to Adler: "Advocacy in support of those in need has become a personal as well as professional pursuit for me. Since I was elected president of FLEOA in 2008, I've made workers' compensation a priority for FLEOA. From 2008 up to the congressional hearing date, I would routinely hear from and communicate with injured members and their spouses. It was disheartening listening to their stories and how their heroic deeds were summarily discarded by incompetent, indifferent government bureaucrats."

Finally, Adler noted: "I'm not an overly religious person, but I believe God built us to be resilient. He gave us the padding on our backside so when we land on it, we can bounce back up. When things don't go according to plan, it makes sense that you'll feel discouraged. Accept the presence of these feelings as natural, and not debilitating, and then take a deep breath and fight on."

RX: PRESCRIPTIONS FOR FOLLOWING THE MORAL COMPASS

You will recall from Chapter One that Albert Bandura has described four ways in which you can increase what he calls personal self-efficacy, i.e., your belief in your own ability to be an effective agent of change. We adapted and then applied his four-part formula as a prescription for how to increase your sense of active optimism, discussed in that same chapter. We will continue to use his scientifically formulated approach in this chapter on following the moral compass. Let's start using Albert Bandura's approach to acquiring new behavior.

Let's review some specific prescriptions for following the four points of the moral compass.

Rx 1: Success and the Self-Fulfilling Prophecy Reinforce the Moral Compass

Act with your moral compass in mind. When you do things successfully, that success creates a belief that you can have further successes. If you believe you can follow a moral compass in life, then you will. Success begets success.

The foundations for the law of effect were published by psychologist Edward L. Thorndike in 1898. The law of effect states that if a desired or pleasant outcome (reward) results from some intentional or even unintentional action, the likelihood of that action recurring is increased. Similarly, if an unpleasant outcome (punishment) results from some action, the likelihood of that action recurring is decreased.

While society should strive to reward people for doing the right thing, that form of external reward does not always occur. Rather, in the final analysis, we should strive to have honesty, integrity, fidelity, and ethical behavior become internally rewarding. Thus, we should strive for actions consistent with following the moral compass to become rewarding in and of themselves. To know you have done the right thing and to have that realization be the highest form of reward you can receive is an admirable goal that epitomizes the height of maturity and responsibility. This characteristic was palpable among the U.S. Navy SEALs we observed.

HOMEWORK

Pick one thing you can do, starting next Monday, that will help you make your moral compass become internally/intrinsically rewarding. Write it here:

Now send yourself an email as a reminder.

Rx 2: Following the Moral Compass Vicariously—
Observing and Setting Valued Norms

When you watch other people act with virtue, it increases the likelihood that you will act that way too. It serves to create a norm for you to aspire to. It helps create a desired virtuous culture. Surround yourself with people who have chosen honesty, integrity, fidelity, and ethical conduct.

The broken windows theory is a powerful concept for you to consider in the quest to follow the moral compass. In social psychology, the broken windows theory asserts that if a neighborhood doesn't fix its broken windows and graffiti, its residents will experience a continuation and even escalation of crime and violence.

James Q. Wilson and George L. Kelling described the theory in the March 1982 issue of *Atlantic Weekly*. According to the authors, if a building has a few windows broken without repair, there is a tendency for people to break more windows, with an eventual escalation to greater damage. The same can be said for graffiti, litter, and perhaps even violent crime. Graffiti that goes unattended seems to predict more graffiti. Litter that goes unattended predicts more littering. And violence that goes unaddressed predicts the development of a culture of violence.

At the same time, there is a decay in the motivation for people to want to do the right thing such as fix windows, clean graffiti, pick up litter, and address violence. A "why bother?" attitude soon develops. According to the broken windows theory, undesirable behavior, when unaddressed, becomes the norm and serves as an example of acceptable behavior, thus predicting further undesirable behavior and social malaise.

On the other hand, when broken windows are quickly fixed,

when graffiti is quickly cleaned, when litter is quickly picked up, and when violence is quickly responded to, subsequent graffiti and crime begin to decline. When the broken windows theory was applied to New York City and Boston, there were dramatic declines in crime and vandalism and an overall improvement in the quality of life. This is the power of establishing, promoting through example, and following desired social norms. This is the power of vicarious learning.

So when it comes to following the moral compass, observe and emulate those who are honest, possess integrity, are faithful, and practice ethical behavior—it's contagious.

HOMEWORK

Pick one thing you can do, starting next Monday, that will help you follow the moral compass vicariously. Write it here:

_____

_____

_____

Now send yourself an email as a reminder.

Rx 3: Following the Moral Compass with the Encouragement and Support of Others

If you live and/or work in an environment where people are consistently and unwaveringly supportive of you and the virtuous goals you seek, you will feel empowered and capable of acting in a virtuous manner.

Psychologists have discovered that your peer group (the group of people you live and work with) is a powerful influence on your life. If you have teenage children, you know this to be true. What we sometimes forget is that the power of the peer group persists beyond our teenage years. Make a conscious effort to associate with people you believe to be of high moral caliber. You will learn from them.

But this prescription goes beyond vicarious learning. It involves active and conspicuous support. The key is making sure that group members are willing to actively support one another. You will gain strength. You will be more inclined to try again in the face of failure, and to see setbacks as temporary. Verbal support is a good thing, but supportive actions from others are better.

HOMEWORK

Pick one thing you can do, starting next Monday, that will help you follow the moral compass using social support. Write it here:

_____

_____

_____

Now send yourself an email as a reminder.

Rx 4: Following the Moral Compass Through Self-Control

Learning to control your own impulsive urges and tendencies to take the easy way out will pay big dividends in that you will accrue a better sense of control and the subsequent belief that you can achieve anything you aspire to. Remember, it's easy to fall prey to temptations of dishonesty when you are in the abyss.

Self-control is imperative in our quest to follow the moral compass. Here are two simple suggestions that will help control impulsive urges to act dishonestly and behave unethically: Just do it! and Just say no!

In 1988, the Nike athletic apparel company coined the phrase "Just do it" as an advertising slogan. Since then the term has become a virtual cultural icon for overcoming hesitation and procrastination.

Sometimes following the moral compass can be fraught with overanalysis and procrastination. When such times arise, you must "Just do it!" When you are faced with a moral dilemma, "Just do it . . . do the right thing!" Avoid paralysis-by-analysis syndrome. Avoid intellectualizations. "Just do it!" The fact that you know you did the proper thing will allow you to sleep well at night, and you will not have to worry about looking over your shoulder. You will feel good about yourself and what you did. It will be easier the next time you face a similar dilemma. Remember golfer Brian Davis, who called a penalty on himself and thereby lost a major golf tournament? Yes, he lost the tournament, but he gained far more in respect and admiration than he lost that day.

In the 1980s there was an anti-drug-abuse advertising campaign that was part of the national War on Drugs. One of the key slogans of this campaign was "Just say no!" The origin of the phrase can be traced to then-First Lady Nancy Reagan. Mrs. Reagan was visiting Longfellow Elementary School in Oakland, California, in 1982. A student asked her what to do if someone offered her drugs. Mrs. Reagan responded, "Just say no." So we say to you, when tempted to act dishonestly, "Just say no." When tempted to act unfaithfully, "Just say no." When urged to act unethically, "Just say no." Make a simple promise to yourself and those you care for. Simply say, "I will never do anything that will hurt my family, my friends, or those who depend on me."

HOMEWORK

Pick one thing you can do, starting next Monday, that will help you follow the moral compass through the practice of self-control. Write it here:

_____

_____

_____

Now send yourself an email as a reminder.

CHAPTER 4

RELENTLESS TENACITY: TRY, TRY AGAIN

What is tenacity? Think of it as perseverance, as steady persistence in a purposeful course of action, especially in spite of difficulties, adversity, or discouragement. As we read the lessons of history and spoke to resilient people, the theme of tenacity was undeniable. Before examining tenacity, however, let's review where we are at this point in the book.

In Chapter One we discussed active optimism, an attitude that goes beyond a belief that things will turn out well. It's the belief that you can make things turn out well. Based on an optimistic belief, the decision to get back on your feet becomes easier. The decision to act is an essential aspect of rebounding from adversity. Action is essential.

Despite temptations to the contrary, the course you choose to rebound from adversity should be one that is plotted using a moral compass. It makes addressing difficult decisions easier. Once the decision to act has been made, armed with an optimist vision and a moral compass to guide you, you must be persistent. Around 1930, Calvin Coolidge, who had been the 30th president of the United States, is credited with having authored one of the most famous endorsements of the trait of persistence. It was published in a pamphlet by the New York Life Insurance Co. as motivation for its sales agents:

Nothing in the world can take the place of Persistence. Talent will not; nothing is more common than unsuccessful men with talent. Genius will not; unrewarded genius is almost a proverb. Education will not; the world is full of educated derelicts. Persistence and determination alone are omnipotent. The slogan 'Press On' has solved and always will solve the problems of the human race.

SELF-ASSESSMENT #4

Directions: Circle the answer that best describes how strongly you agree with the following statements.

1. *Persistence is more important than talent in determining success.*
   1—Strongly disagree
   2—Disagree
   3—Agree
   4—Strongly agree

2. *Tenacity will eventually erode all barriers to success.*
   1—Strongly disagree
   2—Disagree

3—Agree

4—Strongly agree

3. *People give up too quickly when attempting something challenging.*

1—Strongly disagree

2—Disagree

3—Agree

4—Strongly agree

4. *Most people seem to lack perseverance as a work ethic.*

1—Strongly disagree

2—Disagree

3—Agree

4—Strongly agree

5. *Rewards in life should be earned not given.*

1—Strongly disagree

2—Disagree

3—Agree

4—Strongly agree

This self-assessment is not a clinical diagnostic tool. It is simply a survey designed to motivate you to think about your attitudes concerning your work ethic and tenacity. When you have completed the survey, add up the numbers next to the answers you have circled for items #1–5. The lowest score you can have is 5 and the highest is 20. The higher your score, the more tenacious you are likely to be. Now let's learn more about tenacity and its role in human resilience.

THE BEST PLAN FOR SUCCESSFUL RESILIENCE:
TENACIOUS DEFIANCE

*Many of life's failures are people who did not realize how close they were
to success when they gave up.*

— Thomas A. Edison

Failure is simply not an option, resilient people will say. So when
we speak of tenacious defiance of failure, no name in world history
resonates more than Winston Churchill, prime minister of Great
Britain from 1940 to 1945 and again from 1951 to 1955.

On September 1, 1939, the army of Nazi Germany invaded Po-
land, initiating World War II. Great Britain declared war on Germany on September 3, 1939. Following the resignation of Neville
Chamberlain on May 10, 1940, Churchill became prime minister.

At that time, the war was not going well. According to Jon Meacham's 2003 bestseller, *Franklin and Winston: An Intimate Portrait of
an Epic Friendship*, U.S. President Franklin Roosevelt was con-
cerned about the resolve of the British as they faced an impending
German invasion. Churchill was aware of his concern, and in spring
1940 sent Roosevelt a telegram in which he stated, "Our intention
is, whatever happens, to fight on to the end in this Island . . . but in
no conceivable circumstances will we consent to surrender." Shortly
thereafter the British future dramatically darkened. More than
300,000 troops were evacuated from Dunkirk, France, to avoid an-
nihilation at the hands of advancing German forces.

In response to this potentially devastating defeat, and reiterat-
ing his constant theme of perseverance, Churchill famously stated:

"We shall fight in France, we shall fight on the seas and oceans,
we shall fight with growing confidence and growing strength in

the air, we shall defend our island, whatever the cost may be, we shall fight on the beaches, we shall fight on the landing grounds, we shall fight in the fields and in the streets, we shall fight in the hills; we shall never surrender."

By October 29, 1941, the military forces of Nazi Germany had control of Europe, but not Great Britain. Churchill visited his alma mater, the Harrow School, to give an address. In one of his most memorable speeches, he underscored the theme of tenacious defiance once again. "Never give in," he said. "Never give in. Never, never, never, never—in nothing, great or small, large or petty—never give in, except to convictions of honour and good sense. Never yield to force. Never yield to the apparently overwhelming might of the enemy."

In 1963, President John Kennedy, borrowing from Edward R. Murrow's 1942 observation, said of Churchill, "He mobilized the English language and sent it into battle." Indeed, because of Great Britain's stubborn resistance in the face of unrelenting bombing campaigns, the German commanders soon abandoned the planned invasion of Great Britain. At that point, the tide of war changed.

When some people are told they cannot succeed, they give up. When others are told they cannot succeed, they become tenaciously defiant. Pessimism and rejection may be found in your professional life as well as in your personal life. Garry Bonelli and Patrick "Pat" Rummerfield know this well.

REAR ADMIRAL GARRY BONELLI

Born in 1949, Rear Admiral Garry Bonelli, a U.S. Navy SEAL, served as the ninth force commander of the Naval Special Warfare Command (NSW) and currently serves as commissioner of the San Diego Unified Port District. He is also chairman of the Navy SEAL Foundation.

Raised in the Bronx in New York City during the tumultuous 1960s and believing he was soon to be drafted after dropping out of college, he enlisted in the U.S. Navy in 1968. Bonelli made two ground combat deployments in Vietnam as a Navy Frogman with Underwater Demolition Team 12. In 1990, Bonelli was mobilized in support of Operations Desert Shield and Desert Storm. He has the distinction of being the first and only reservist ever to command an active-duty SEAL team.

Recalled to active duty again in 2006, Bonelli served as the chief of staff, then deputy commander, and ultimately the force commander of NSW. As the ninth NSW force commander, Admiral Bonelli led a 9,000-person force of SEALs, special boat operators, mission specialists, and civilian subject-matter experts. The command is a $1 billion enterprise that develops strategy, doctrine, and tactics for NSW operations worldwide. Bonelli had 45 years of combined active and reserve service when he retired in 2013.

Bonelli's naval career is a remarkable story of relentless tenacity and determination in which he rose from seaman apprentice to admiral. He would ultimately lead all U.S. Navy special operators as the force commander of NSW. In the process, he would marry, raise a family, and enjoy successful business and public service careers.

After enlisting, he was sent to navy boot camp at the recruit training center outside Chicago. Bonelli recalled that in less than 24 hours, a recruit learns the most important person in your navy life is a chief petty officer, capable of having a significant influence on the trajectory of your career in the navy.

As he was mulling what aptitude he might have for the navy, a navy chief petty officer came into the recruits' open bay barracks and showed an old 16-mm film depicting men scuba diving. The chief was seeking volunteers for something called SEAL training. Bonelli raised his hand and volunteered. However, he first had to pass a rigorous battery of physical stamina tests, such as distance running, swimming, and a number of body-numbing calisthenics.

He made it through most of the physical tests but failed the timed 1.5-mile distance run by a mere few seconds. Confronted with failure, Bonelli requested that he immediately be allowed to do the run again—confident that he could run faster. The instructor staff allowed him to run again, knowing it would be nearly impossible to improve his run time without rest. Bonelli took off running and finished the entire 1.5-mile run 55 seconds slower than before. However, the instructor staff was so impressed with his determination that they accepted him into the special unit.

The young recruits in the underwater demolition team/ SEAL boot camp company were immediately told they were special. Following a mere nine weeks in boot camp, Bonelli's special company graduated with black berets and parachute boots instead of the traditional navy blue sailor uniforms topped by "dixie cup" hats. Indeed, Bonelli and most of the members of the unit thought they were special. Little did they realize that the intense and brutal SEAL selection and training pipeline had just begun.

Arriving in San Diego, California, in late 1968, at Coro-

nado Naval Amphibious Base, he would begin a nine-
month test of mind, body, and soul to complete the arduous
basic underwater demolition/SEAL (BUD/S) training with
its notorious "Hell Week." Many consider BUD/S the most
difficult military training in the world. Today, only one in
five young men are selected to start BUD/S, and after more
than a year of training, only one in four candidates gradu-
ates to become a SEAL.

Bonelli was not prepared to start BUD/S Class #50 in
comparison to his classmates. After all, his training class of
130-plus students included college Division 1A athletes. In
fact, there were men already in the SEAL teams who were
medaled Olympians.

The first four weeks of BUD/S training didn't go well
for candidate Bonelli. Every hour of every day proved
daunting for him. Even the short jogs to the chow hall for
brief respites were difficult. He was part of what the instructor staff called the goon squad, which consisted of students barely meeting the intense physical demands being
placed on them.

To drive home how miserably the goon squad performed, the instructor staff would order members to wade
into the frigid Pacific Ocean surf for a dunking, then roll in
beach sand while attempting to finish timed distance runs—
euphemistically referred to as "conditioning hikes." The
pressure on goon-squad members to drop out was always
intense.

By the start of training week five—Hell Week—most of
his classmates had indeed been dropped from training at

their own request. Bonelli bonded with and respected his fellow trainees; he desperately wanted to hang in there with them to get through Hell Week together. Sticking with his fellow trainees, and exhibiting his own tenacity and determination, helped him survive the first phase of BUD/S. With Hell Week behind him, Bonelli was feeling like he might actually complete the months-long training that led to graduation. But a greater, unforeseen challenge was only weeks away.

Several times a week as part of training, students were required to navigate their way through a torturous obstacle course on Coronado's Silver Strand beach. As one of the slower students, Bonelli was pushing himself when he fell off of an obstacle called the skyscraper, dropping 30 feet and breaking his collarbone.

He had two choices: request to be dropped from BUD/S and reassigned to a regular navy fleet job or start BUD/S training all over from day one. Bonelli wanted to serve his country as a SEAL, and he wanted to serve with his classmates who were all challenged to achieve the same goal.

Refusing to quit, he was rolled back to BUD/S Class #51 to start training over from day one. That's *two* Hell Weeks, and a broken collarbone in between. He would graduate with BUD/S Class #51 in 1969 and immediately deploy to the western Pacific, finding himself in Vietnam in ground combat.

Following his second combat tour, Bonelli was released from active duty and became a "plank owner" (a member of the commissioning crew) of the first NSW reserve unit.

While completing his master of science degree in mass communications in 1976, he received a direct commission in the U.S. Navy Reserve. During the ensuing years, he served as the commanding officer of eight SEAL reserve units.

Bonelli was mobilized in 1990 during the first Gulf War in support of Operations Desert Shield and Desert Storm. He served as the commanding officer of SEAL Team 5.

More recently, Admiral Bonelli was installed as the volunteer chairman of the board of directors of the Navy SEAL Foundation. The foundation (at navysealfoundation.org) is the nonprofit umbrella benevolent organization providing immediate and ongoing support to SEALs and their families.

As the chairman, Admiral Bonelli sets the strategic agenda and guides the execution of the foundation. He works with donors and military leaders to ensure the foundation is meeting current needs and anticipating future requirements of his teammates and their families.

Bonelli told us he has no regrets, indicating he has treasured the experiences that have shaped him. "I wouldn't do anything different. Every day has been special." Looking back on his initial BUD/S training days, he said, "Whether hot or cold, wet and sandy, exhausted, just plain miserable, or scared out of my wits, it was a blast." He noted that his lifetime of experiences in and out of the military have been guided by the SEAL ethos instilled in him as a teenager. Thus we see that tenacity can compensate for the lack of natural strength.

PATRICK "PAT" RUMMERFIELD

Winston Churchill is credited with saying, "If you are going through hell, keep going." Patrick Rummerfield found himself in hell, and he kept going. Rummerfield (born September 7, 1953) is not only a living example of tenacity, he is a living miracle. Rummerfield is the world's first fully recovered, functioning quadriplegic.

Rummerfield was born into an abusive family situation that resulted in him being removed from his home and placed in an orphanage. The orphanage taught him tenacity and toughness. "My background is one of a fighter," he told us. "Growing up in an orphanage, I had to fight. I've always been a fighter. 'Quit' isn't in my vocabulary. I learned at an early age that if you wanted something you had to go for it, you had to fight for it. Later, I was adopted at age 7. My father taught me the importance of having mental toughness in any kind of disabling injury or anything, like divorce, going bankrupt. . . . [S]taying focused and not dwelling on negatives is the key."

On September 20, 1974, at age 21, Rummerfield and a friend, in the midst of his bachelor party, were in a car accident while traveling 135 miles per hour. Rummerfield's car left the road and hit a ditch with such force that the passenger's seat was sheared away from the car on impact.

"We hit at such a velocity that I went halfway through the windshield and popped my right eye out of its socket, sliced my scalp off, broke my neck in four places [vertebrae C-3, 4, 5, and 6] and broke just about every bone in my body.

At C-4, 85 percent of my spinal cord was severed. My initial evaluation indicated that I would only have 72 hours to live. A week later they said that I had beaten a billion-to-one odds but that I would be quadriplegic from the neck down for rest of my life. In the 1970s, they put quads in nursing homes . . . [L]ife expectancy was only three to five years.

"One of the lowest points for me after the accident was not being able to move anything. How was I going to cope? The worst thing is how am I going to take care of myself, who will take care of me, financially? These questions run through your mind late at night. I remember watching the night janitor buff the floor. I know three months earlier, I would have been thinking that poor guy, life dealt him a rough hand. . . . [N]ow, lying in the bed, I would have given anything to be buffing the floor at 1 in the morning."

Rummerfield's comeback began when he was lying in bed thinking about how much he would like to play basketball, and how he would love to drive a race car. At that point his toe moved. Against his physician's advice, Rummerfield insisted on beginning a regimen of intensive daily physical therapy.

Rummerfield has not only recovered the ability to use his arms and legs, but in October 1992, he competed in an Ironman triathlon. And there's more. In February 1997, he became one of only 82 people in history to complete the Antarctica Marathon. Later, he was on the rehabilitation team that worked with paralyzed actor Christopher Reeve.

Today Pat Rummerfield works on the staff of the Kennedy Krieger Institute's International Center for Spinal

Cord Injury at the Johns Hopkins Medical Institutions. He also gives presentations on spinal cord rehabilitation, as well as resilience.

So what was the key to Rummerfield's recovery?

"I kept telling myself that everything was going to be OK and God has a plan for me. This isn't the end. I refused to give up trying. I kept working and working toward my goals, knowing eventually I would achieve them. They might be generic goals, meaning I might not be able to win the Ironman, but I finished one. I'll take a generic victory any day."

Is there a lesson to be learned about human resilience from the life of Pat Rummerfield?

"The only time we fail," he said, "is when we quit. You never give up, you never give in, and with time you will develop an iron will. From that you will always win. I tell myself that over and over again. You can choose to be sad. I was taught early on by the gentleman that adopted me, don't waste time on negative thoughts or actions.

"Thinking 'woe is me' isn't going to get you where you want to be. You have to keep telling yourself to move forward. No matter how dark it gets or how unlikely it looks, keep pushing yourself. In a marathon, you come around the bend and see the finish line. Gotta keep pushing yourself until you reach the finish line. I will spend my time now helping others, increasing the quality of life for others that aren't as fortunate as I am. That's what I've been doing the last 40 years and will do the next 40."

TENACITY: SOMETIMES THE JOURNEY IS
MORE IMPORTANT THAN THE DESTINATION

"I will never quit. I persevere and thrive on adversity. If knocked down, I will get back up, every time. I will draw on every remaining ounce of strength to protect my teammates and to accomplish our mission. I am never out of the fight." This passage, adapted from the U.S. Navy SEAL Ethos, could easily describe the life of Cal Ripken Jr.

CAL RIPKEN JR.

Cal Ripken Jr., born on August 24, 1960, nicknamed "the Iron Man," played 21 seasons of professional baseball for the Baltimore Orioles. His last season was 2001.

Ripken is considered one of the best shortstops to ever play the game. Early in his career, he moved from playing third base to shortstop. At six feet four inches and 225 pounds, he broke the traditional mold for a shortstop, a position typically reserved for smaller and faster players. Nevertheless, Ripken won two Golden Glove awards for his defensive play. He was twice named the American League's Most Valuable Player and chosen 19 times as an American League All-Star, ultimately becoming the prototype for the new-era professional shortstop.

Even with all of these accolades, Ripken will no doubt be best remembered for setting the Major League Baseball record for consecutive games played. On September 6, 1995, Ripken played his 2,131st consecutive game, breaking the record held by Lou Gehrig. Baseball fans voted this event as the "most memorable moment" in an MLB.com poll. Perhaps for the love of the game, Ripken voluntarily ended his 17-year streak at 2,632 games in 1998. Even though he could have extended the streak far longer, he felt it was in the best interest of the team and the game to give younger players a chance to develop. He retired after the 2001 season. That season, Ripken was named the All-Star Game MVP and honored with the Commissioner's Historic Achievement Award.

Even with such an amazing career, there were low points. Perhaps the lowest came in 1988. Ripken's father, Cal Ripken Sr., a longtime Orioles coach, was finally given a chance to manage the team in 1987 and 1988. But after six consecutive losses to begin the 1988 season, the Orioles fired Ripken Sr. His son felt a sense of disappointment, if not betrayal, from the firing. So distressing was this period in his life that he considered leaving the Orioles and playing for another baseball team. In an interview, Ripken later told us:

"I believe that if Dad was let go closer to the end of the season and I didn't have the time to evaluate the situation, I very well could have ended up playing elsewhere. However, as the season went on, I had time to really look closely at what was important to me and my family, and at the end of the day I opted to move on and stay with the Orioles. Dad never stopped encouraging us to be the best we could be, and once the emotions of the situation calmed down it was easier for me to see that at that time we were not a very strong team and we were just starting a lengthy rebuilding process."

Ironically, the Orioles went on to lose 15 more consecutive games under the new manager. But after 21 consecutive
losses, the team rebounded. The following year the Orioles
played for the division championship.

As testament that the events of 1988 had a profound effect on Ripken, he wrote a 2007 children's book, *The Longest
Season*. When we asked why he wrote the book, Ripken replied: "I thought it was a great subject for a book and kids
can learn so much from the takeaways of going through a
challenging time. Rather than crumble and fold, I wanted
kids to read the book and know that there is always light at
the end of the tunnel. . . . For us, that team really came together and just a year later we battled for the division title
right down to the last weekend of the season. I just think
that, as hard as it is when you are going through a tough
period, you have to take some positives away from that and
persevere. Persevering builds strength and character that
will serve you at a later time."

Even the most amazing of accomplishments will have its
detractors. As mentioned earlier, Ripken broke Lou Gehrig's "Ironman" streak of 2,130 consecutive baseball games
played. He went on to play in a total of 2,632 consecutive
games. It will come as a surprise to many that Ripken was
actually criticized for the remarkable reliability and tenacity
that went into breaking Gehrig's record. Some viewed the
streak as self-serving because Ripken was not always playing well.

Those critics miss the point completely. Resilience based
on perseverance is all about trying your best regardless of

how you feel, regardless of what your critics say, and regardless how compelling the urge to simply quit, or take a day off, may be. The "Ironman" streak was not just about one player's tenacity but about his love of his team, his city, and his game. There's no doubt in Ripken's mind that his career would have lasted longer and his stats been even better if he had not played every day—if he'd rested when tired and healed when injured. Resilient tenacity is all about reliability and perseverance, especially when it hurts.

Today Ripken is president and CEO of Ripken Baseball Inc. *Fortune* has referred to him as the "Iron Businessman," having become the prototype for a successful career in business following a career in professional sports. Although Ripken Baseball owns three minor league teams, its focus appears to be in youth baseball. The value of giving back is at the heart of Ripken Baseball and at the heart of Ripken the person. He is intimately involved in numerous charities in his community and throughout the United States, most noteworthy the Cal Ripken, Sr. Foundation.

Never a flashy player on the field, Ripken was the embodiment of ironclad reliability. In personal interactions one is struck by his humility, sincerity, and compassion.

Ripken is the type of professional athlete who kids can look up to. He's the embodiment of the tenacity that predicts extraordinary success.

In his 2007 book, *Get in the Game*, Ripken acknowledges the power of perseverance and presents it as a core value that predicts success in all aspects of life. He lists eight elements of perseverance:

1. *The Right Values*—Be reliable. Come to work ready to work, focusing on your job, not someone else's.

2. *A Strong Will to Succeed*—The drive to be successful is the fuel of perseverance.

3. *Love What You Do*—You will be less obsessed about performance per se. But your performance will come naturally, not as a result of fear or coercion.

4. *Preparation*—There's an old saying in sports: "You play the way you practice." Practice is seldom fun, but it's the best predictor of your performance when it really counts.

5. *Anticipation*—Anticipate problems before they occur. Situational awareness is critical to all aspects of life.

6. *Trusting Relationships*—Most aspects of your life involve teamwork. Develop constructive, supportive relationships on which you can rely in times of adversity.

7. *Life Management*—Some people believe your personal life and work life are separate. They aren't. Each affects the other. The totality of your life is a balancing act. Find the balance that works best for you. But don't fall prey to the delusion that you can harm one to benefit the other. Harm to one harms the other.

8. *The Courage of Your Convictions*—If your convictions are firmly based and well-honed then stick to them. Have the courage to resist the majority opinion if you think it's wrong. And yes, you must be

thick skinned. Understand that people will criticize you if they disagree with you, are jealous of you, or if they simply are unhappy with themselves.

ROY McAVOY

Cal Ripken Jr.'s story is largely one of remarkable success. Roy McAvoy's is a fictional story of failure that exemplifies when the process is more important than the outcome.

Oh, you've never heard of Roy McAvoy? The movie *Tin Cup* is a 1996 romantic comedy that stars Kevin Costner as Roy McAvoy, a hapless golf professional giving lessons at a run-down driving range in West Texas. In an effort to attract the affection of a woman, McAvoy qualifies to play in the U.S. Open.

The movie builds to a crescendo as McAvoy is tied for the championship approaching the last hole of the tournament. After he makes a good drive into the fairway on his first shot, his caddy advises him to play it safe and make a short approach shot to get close to the green and then take another shot in order to put his ball on the green. This would force a playoff for the championship. McAvoy ignores his caddy's advice and attempts to put his ball on the green with his second shot. His ball hits the green, but then rolls into the water. McAvoy takes out another ball and attempts the same shot with the same result. He does this until he has only one ball left. On his 12th shot he puts the ball in the cup. But it's too late. McAvoy has lost his chance to make history by winning the U.S. Open.

In his humiliation, he realizes that his tenacity was poorly timed and ill-placed—until the woman who is the object of his affection offers her interpretation of what seems like his irresponsible actions. She says, "Five years from now nobody will remember who won or lost, but they're gonna remember your 12!" And all was not lost on the course either. By finishing in the top 15, McAvoy automatically qualified to play in the U.S. Open the following year.

The real-life journey of Cal Ripken Jr. and the fictional journey of Roy McAvoy show us that while the end result is certainly important, sometimes the journey itself counts even more. In a world with a singular—and sometimes self-destructive—fixation on outcome, keep in mind that how you achieved the outcome matters. The rare attributes of reliability and tenacity will make you stand out. They are also likely to engender the support of others who wish to contribute to the successful outcome that a tenacious journey deserves.

WHEN TO MOVE ON

When is tenacity no longer useful? The answer would appear to be: when the tenacious effort toward any goal becomes more of a liability than an asset; when resources dedicated in one direction are better reallocated in another.

Roy McAvoy's actions may seem like a stubborn, irresponsible obsession. After his first failed shot, some would argue that he'd have been wise to play it safe with his next shot. The best-case scenario would have been a third-place finish. But McAvoy, while failing epically, actually redefined success. Sometimes the process becomes more important than the outcome.

When does Cal Ripken Jr. decide to end his streak of consecutive games? One could argue the streak should have ended when it jeopardized his health, or perhaps when he became more of a liability than an asset to his team. But that didn't happen. Ripken continued to play well and to contribute to his team's performance. Oh, and he increased attendance. Everywhere he played, even after he broke Gehrig's record, people would come out to see a man who was already one of the great legends of the game of baseball.

So when does tenacity become self-defeating? The answer is: when continued tenacious effort creates more problems than can be resolved once a successful outcome is achieved.

RX: PRESCRIPTIONS FOR BUILDING PERSONAL TENACITY

Both Cal Ripken Jr. and Pat Rummerfield agree that tenacity is an attitude that comes from within. They further agree that it can be learned.

Rx 1: Choose a Goal and Practice Tenacity

Tenacity becomes self-sustaining when perseverant actions are rewarded. Success in the wake of tenacity is rewarding. It says all of the tenacious hard work can pay off. Choose a goal for which the best predictor of success is simply tenacious adherence to a plan of action. Mobilize the one thing over which you have complete control: how hard you will work to achieve your desired goal. Then go for it.

Rx 2: Observe Tenacious Role Models

Tenacity is increased when we see or read about others who over-
came great barriers to be successful using tenacious defiance. Find
tenacious role models. Study history; it's full of examples of tenacious defiance of failure. In this book we have intentionally combined stories from the past with those of the present to point out
one consistent theme: the power of tenacity.

Rx 3: Find People to Support Your Tenacity

Perhaps another powerful theme that emerges from the stories of
Winston Churchill, Cal Ripken Jr., Pat Rummerfield, and Garry
Bonelli is that tenacity in the wake of adversity is aided by the support of others. Churchill needed the support of the United States if
Britain was going to survive the war with Nazi Germany. In his
book *Franklin and Winston*, Jon Meacham quotes Churchill's son
Randolph's recollection of a conversation with his father in which
Randolph asked how Britain could possibly defeat Germany. The
elder Churchill replied, "I shall drag the United States in." It was
the cohesiveness of Ripken's Oriole teammates that ultimately led
to a winning season following his "longest season." During Rummerfield's rehabilitation, it was the support of his medical "dream
team" that allowed him to learn to walk again. In the case of
Bonelli, the support of his immediate supervisor and later his
teammates was essential to his future success.

HOMEWORK

Pick one thing you can do, starting next Monday, that will help you become more tenacious. Write it here:

_____

_____

_____

Now send yourself an email as a reminder.

CHAPTER 5

GAIN STRENGTH FROM THE SUPPORT OF OTHERS

"I humbly serve as a guardian to my fellow Americans always ready to defend those who are unable to defend themselves. I do not advertise the nature of my work, nor seek recognition for my actions. I voluntarily accept the inherent hazards of my profession, placing the welfare and security of others before my own." These lines, adapted from the U.S. Navy SEAL Ethos, exemplify the nature of interpersonal support within a highly cohesive group.

SELF-ASSESSMENT #5

Directions: Circle the answer that best describes how strongly you agree with the following statements.

1. *I have a supportive family.*

    1—Strongly disagree

    2—Disagree

    3—Agree

    4—Strongly agree

2. *I have supportive friends.*

    1—Strongly disagree

    2—Disagree

    3—Agree

    4—Strongly agree

3. *I have a supportive work environment.*

    1—Strongly disagree

    2—Disagree

    3—Agree

    4—Strongly agree

4. *I believe I should always consider the option of seeking assistance in order to manage problems and crises.*

    1—Strongly disagree

    2—Disagree

    3—Agree

    4—Strongly agree

5. *I don't hesitate asking for help.*

    1—Strongly disagree

    2—Disagree

    3—Agree

    4—Strongly agree

This self-assessment is not a clinical diagnostic tool. It is simply a survey designed to motivate you to think about your attitudes about interpersonal support. When you have completed the survey, simply add up the numbers next to the answers you have circled for items #1–5. The lowest score you can have is 5, the highest is 20. The higher your score, the more supportive resources you are likely to have and use. Let's read more about resilience and interpersonal support.

In Chapter One, we discussed active optimism and how it can lead to the powerful phenomenon of a self-fulfilling prophecy. In Chapter Two, we argued that optimism is not enough. In order to bounce back when life has knocked you down, you must be decisive and act. In Chapter Three, we introduced a notion that may make difficult decisions easier: We argued that your ascent from the darkness of the abyss is made easier when you use the moral compass to find your direction. In Chapter Four, we introduced what we believe is the single greatest predictor of success in virtually any human endeavor: tenacity. Here in Chapter Five, we review the support of others, what Colin Powell called a "force multiplier."

It was Aristotle who first claimed that the entirety of a group was greater than the sum of its parts. This notion, termed *synergy*, is the theoretical basis for the putative superiority of group decision making and the creation of functional work groups (the principle of the division of labor) in virtually every industry. But this notion is an oversimplification, and its ramifications are far too important to simply accept without more granular scrutiny. It's not the group per se—the mere aggregation of individuals—in which the strength lies, but in its coherency and its members' willingness to contribute to one another and to the collective well-being.

THE POWER OF INTERPERSONAL COHESION AND SUPPORT

Interpersonal cohesion refers to the tendency of the members of a group to identify with other members, share values, and provide support in times of distress. Interpersonal support is believed to be the single best predictor of human resilience. It really is whom you know that counts when you are making your comeback from, or even avoiding a descent into, the abyss, psychologically or physically.

According to Martin Nowak, professor of biology at Harvard University, socially cohesive and supportive groups are likely to be stronger and more resilient. He notes:

> Individuals may perform selfless acts for the greater good, as opposed to abetting a single peer. Recognition of this mechanism dates back to Darwin himself, who observed in his 1871 book *The Descent of Man* that "a tribe including many members who . . . were always ready to aid one another, and to sacrifice themselves for the common good, would be victorious over most other tribes; and this would be natural selection."

Social cohesion and interpersonal support have wide implications for the human experience. The field of psychosomatic medicine is the study of the effects of psychological and social factors on physical health.

The seminal integrative text of the modern era, written by J. P. Henry and P. M. Stephens in 1977, notes that bonding between group members, group ritual behavior, shared beliefs, altruism, and a propensity for mutual aid are all remarkably protective and resilience-enhancing factors against all manner of external threats as well as intrinsically stressful and self-defeating forces for individuals and communities.

Regarding individual health, research suggests that interpersonal connectedness protects against overall mortality, coronary heart disease, immune suppression, and increased stress. In an important meta-analytic review of the effects of loneliness on mortality, data on more than 308,000 subjects was analyzed. The researchers discovered that people with stronger social relationships had a 50 percent increased likelihood of survival than those with weaker social relationships. In fact, interpersonal support was two to three times as powerful a predictor of survival as was dieting, physical exercise, or smoking cessation.

THE ROSETO EFFECT

Communities prosper from cohesion and mutual support as well. One of the founding fathers of the field of psychosomatic medicine was Stewart Wolf, a Johns Hopkins–trained physician. While Wolf made many important contributions, one of his greatest was his study of Roseto, Pennsylvania, which is summarized in his 1993 book, *The Power of Clan: The Influences of Human Relationships on Heart Disease*. The book tells the story of the socially cohesive community of Roseto and Wolf's amazing 25-year investigation (1963–1988) of the health of its inhabitants.

Italian immigrants from the Roseto Valfortore region founded Roseto around 1883. The settlers brought with them their village's values, culture, and lifestyle, making Roseto a medical marvel and giving rise to the term the *Roseto Effect*. Wolf found that while the community's inhabitants possessed the same risk factors for heart disease—such as smoking, high-cholesterol diets, and a sedentary lifestyle—as the residents of surrounding towns, the death rate of Roseto residents from heart disease was less than half that in surrounding towns. In addition, Roseto had virtually no crime and no need for government welfare.

Wolf discovered that the protective factor was not in the water, nor the air, but in the people themselves and a remarkably supportive climate that fostered the health, happiness, and success of the community's inhabitants. More specifically, research revealed that social cohesiveness, traditional family values, a family-oriented social structure (where three and even four generations could reside in the same household), and emotional support imparted immunity from heart disease. The people of Roseto shared a strong Italian heritage. They practiced the same religion. They shared a strong sense of community identity and civic pride.

Even more intriguing, the mutually protective social network of Roseto was built on an established standard of values and behavior capable of actually shaping how the brain itself functions. According to Wolf:

"Thus impressions from the environment, and especially from human relationships, immediate and remote, can powerfully shape many cognitive and behavioral aspects of the person. . . . [I]ndividual [amygdaloid] responses to otherwise stressful life experiences may have been muted . . . [by] the interpretive circuits of the brain and consequently the [neuroendocrine] workings of the body."

Unfortunately, with time, the young adults of Roseto embraced the suburban lifestyle of the 1960s. The residents of Roseto slowly abandoned the mutually supportive family-oriented social structure, adopting instead a form of social competitiveness. As they did, the prevalence of heart disease rose. The immunity that a shared identity, mutual values, and social cohesion had afforded was eventually lost, and the rate of deaths from heart disease in Roseto became equal to that of neighboring towns. As one couple declared:

"We are very aggressive to get another job or to earn more money to attain the two-car family. I envy other people. I work hard, so what I do have I'm proud of, and I hope to be able to have more things. I worry about it—I'll be honest."

According to Wolf, the village-style living was abandoned, "construction of new houses began on the edges of the town, large houses, some of them ranch-type with broad green lawns, fountains, and swimming pools. One housewife, after a year in such elegant surroundings, stated: 'I'm sorry we moved. Everything is very modern here, very nice. I have everything I need, except people.'"

A HELPING HAND AT A CRITICAL TIME CAN CHANGE YOUR WORLD

The stories of Donald Tyson and Erika Brannock show the importance of interpersonal support at critical points in our professional and personal lives, respectively. For Tyson, the support of others saved his career. For Brannock, the support of others saved her life.

DONALD GENE TYSON

Donald Gene Tyson, born in Wichita, Kansas, on February 19, 1947, was raised on a small farm in rural Valley Center, 15 miles north of Wichita. His father was a driving rural letter carrier for the U.S. Postal Service, and his mother was a homemaker. Tyson had an identical twin brother, Ronald Dean Tyson.

When Tyson was 9, his father was transferred to Wichita, Kansas, where he continued with the post office, but as a letter carrier who walked his mail route. In addition, his father had a second job parking cars at a local Wichita auto parking company. While Tyson didn't like school, his twin brother was the studious type. In high school, Tyson barely passed. His goal was to leave home and join the U.S. Navy.

When he turned 17, he and a friend quit high school and joined the navy. When he arrived in Kansas City, Missouri, to be inducted, he failed the written entry exam. A navy chief told Tyson to apply to another military service. Tyson adamantly refused. He begged the chief to accept him so he could accompany his friend into the navy. Finally, the chief relented, and Tyson arrived in San Diego, California, in July 1964 to begin training. Tyson later said the chief probably saved his life. He told us, "I would have ended up dead or in jail."

Tyson graduated from boot camp and was assigned to his first duty station at Corry Field, Pensacola, Florida. One night while stationed in Pensacola, he and another shipmate were taken into custody for underage drinking. The shore patrol report was turned over to the division officer, and soon Tyson had his first Captain's Mast (disciplinary hearing) before the base commanding officer. Asked how many beers he had consumed, he replied, "Only one, Sir." The captain ordered Tyson to report to the base rock pile and pound away for four hours as his punishment. Surprisingly, Tyson's division officer ensured that his military record remained absent of any Captain's Mast.

While some might see this incident as insignificant, it wasn't for Tyson. For a second time in his young adult life, an authority figure supported him. Tyson noted, "This 'little' incident turned my life around. I gained respect for great leadership." Tyson learned that resiliency is often predicated upon the support of others. And he learned that great leaders "take care of their own" while insisting on honesty and accountability. From that point forward in his career, Tyson strove for perfection. If others were willing to invest in him, he owed it to them to invest in himself. This meant doing not just good enough, but the best he could.

While assigned to a U.S. naval base in Naples, Italy, Tyson met members of a deployed SEAL team. From that point, his dream was to become a SEAL. There was a significant problem, however, because Tyson, raised in Kansas, had never learned to swim.

Remembering the promise he made to himself in Pensacola, he began by taking swimming lessons. For an entire year, every day he could, Tyson practiced swimming. Against the odds, he was chosen to enter basic training for the SEALs, but a bigger challenge remained. One of the tests was a grueling, open-ocean swim. With some apprehension, but armed with the promise he made to himself,

Tyson entered the water to begin a timed, four-mile, open-ocean swim. Tyson passed the test and ultimately realized his dream of becoming a U.S. Navy SEAL. While continuing his career in naval special warfare as a SEAL, he went on to earn a college degree. He retired after a 20-year career as a lieutenant and former master chief petty officer.

After retiring from the navy, Tyson decided he would continue to protect his country as a special agent and federal air marshal for the Federal Aviation Administration (FAA) Security Division. While on a mission in Pakistan during the Persian Gulf War in 1991, he contracted bacterial endocarditis. This illness necessitated three open-heart surgeries and two aortic-valve replacements. He was hospitalized for 11 months.

When Tyson recovered, he continued to serve his country. The Berlin Wall, which divided East and West Berlin, was dismantled in November 1989, and the Cold War largely ended in 1991. Former residents of Eastern Bloc countries began to move to Western Europe any way they could. One method for gaining access to the West was to hijack an airplane, especially to Sweden, Norway, or Denmark. This means of escaping to the West became popular because even though the hijackers were arrested and sent to prison, they were paid a per diem there that was greater than many made as a working wage in their home countries.

Tyson investigated four to six hijackings per month. The physical demands eventually took their toll. Once again, caring assistance came into play: With the support of the US ambassador, in concert with Cathal "Irish" Flynn, associate administrator for the FAA Security Division and a rear admiral and former SEAL leader, Tyson was retired on the basis of a medical disability in 1995. Most recently, in July 2012, he had his fourth open-heart surgery to repair an ascending aortic aneurysm.

As a young adult in the navy, Tyson learned to appreciate how one's resiliency is based on the support of others. As John Donne wrote in his 1624 *"Meditation 17,"* "No man is an island." At the right time, the right person can change the trajectory of your life—if you are willing to listen. The lesson was repeated for Tyson as a SEAL operator facing life-threatening adversity, where he learned it's all about the mission and the team.

"As a SEAL," Tyson noted, "you are trained and conditioned to maintain a positive mental attitude and look after your teammates. . . . [Y]ou must remain intently focused and disciplined in order to make the decisions that enable you to complete your mission and take care of your men."

Even when his medical condition compelled him to retire, Tyson once again saw how good leaders took care of their people. "Resilience is a matter of attitude," he said. Time and patience are keys. The solutions to many problems in life are often hidden behind a veil of needless urgency, or the blinding emotions of anger, fear, or depression. "The power of prayer," he concluded, "my faith, and my loving wife Cherell have nursed me back to health, and continue to do so."

Tyson's story of resilience exemplifies the power of a supportive, interpersonal presence at key points in your life. It can result in uplifting changes, not only to the trajectory of your life but to your basic attitudes as well.

ERIKA BRANNOCK

Reported to be the oldest annual marathon event in the world, the Boston Marathon is one of the great international sporting events. Founded in 1897, the marathon attracts more than 30,000 racers and 500,000 onlookers each year. On April 15, 2013, in an act of overt terrorism, two pressure-cooker bombs exploded near the marathon finish line. Three people were killed and 264 injured. Twenty-nine-year-old Erika Brannock, a preschool teacher in Baltimore, was among the injured.

Brannock and her sister and brother-in-law were spectators, waiting to see their mother, who was one of the racers, complete the marathon. While looking for a good place to observe the finish, the sisters stopped near the Marathon's 26-mile marker to observe the Newtown Memorial. Brannock recalled that someone moved so they could get closer for a better view. Then at 2:49 p.m. (EDT), she was caught in the bomb blast. Brannock told us:

"All I remember is not being able to hear and falling back slowly. I blacked out for a second, and there were sirens going off, air was cloudy and felt like someone was on top of me. It felt like my knee was twisted. I never heard the actual explosion, but I saw the flashes of orange and thought a transformer had blown. I came to, and it felt like my legs were on fire. From what I gather later and what I saw from pictures, Jeff Bauman's knees were 8 inches from my head (Bauman lost both legs in the explosion). We were a foot from the bomb. My sister was blown away from me with her back to me.

"I tried to get up but couldn't. I reached down, and when I brought my hand up, blood was everywhere. I started to scream my sister and brother-in-law's names. Then my mind seemed to wander somewhere else. I later told people that I had a near-death experience. I thought, 'This is how I am going to die, without my family being here.'

"Then I saw a very bright light and sensed the presence of God. It was a strong comforting presence. I felt energy inside of me or around me like someone was there. I felt like someone was going to help me. I had a conversation with him and said, 'I'm not going now, you aren't going to take me.'

"That's when someone grabbed my hand and she started screaming for someone to help. An off-duty EMT asked for a belt to tie on my leg as a tourniquet. I said, 'Someone needs to call my mom and my brother in law.'

"When they were wheeling me into the ER, I blacked out. They had to resuscitate me because my blood pressure went to 70/10. I asked what happened to my legs? I was told I was really badly injured and my legs were really hurt.

"I woke up next day with a tube in my mouth, and my mom was there. I just started making a motion in the air that I wanted to write. I wrote questions: What happened to my legs? My mom told me they'd had to amputate. I just started crying. There was a lump in my throat. She said, 'You are going to be OK.' She told me that my sister and brother-in-law were OK, but at a different hospital. I asked what they had told my students. I had an idea that this was a day later or so, and she said, 'Don't worry, they told them that you got hurt but that you were going to be OK.' I was moved to critical care with the other survivors.

"At times the recovery has been frustrating. At my lowest point, pain and muscle spasms were almost constant. I remember getting ready for one of my multiple surgeries. I wanted to either live or die, but not continue in this limbo. I broke down and cried. I said, 'I don't know if I will come out of this surgery.' Mom said it was not me talking. I said that I felt defeated.

"I wasn't close to anyone there, and I was miles away from family, friends, and students. My dad came and I was thankful I had my mom. But I often felt defeated and I wanted it all to go away. My mother kept telling me this wasn't me. . . . I'm an optimistic upbeat person. She was right. I changed my attitude then and decided that instead of being miserable, I was going to use humor and sarcasm to get through. But most importantly, I decided I would get through this.

"But it still wasn't easy. I got a bone infection so I had to go in for more surgeries. It messes with you. Around Christmas I hit another low point. I had panic attacks. I finally admitted that I was not OK, and I had to admit that it's all right for me to not be OK, but that it's going to be better and to be patient with myself. I had been patient with two-year-olds. Now I had to be patient with myself."

What does Brannock's story tell us about coming back from the abyss? An optimistic attitude is critical. "It's OK to feel down, just don't stay there," she said. "I say to people, 'Don't refer to me as a victim.' . . . You can't be a victim, you must be a survivor. I choose to be in a positive place. It's important to appreciate the small things in life . . . like when I first stood up and it didn't hurt, and hugging a kid. Focus on what you have, not what you've lost. Yes, I lost my legs, but I am still here. I can still do all that I did before. I just have to get used to doing them a different way."

Perhaps most important to Brannock was the support of others. "I got packages from school. My hospital room was plastered with pictures from kids. I was there for 50 days and never spent a night alone. I was scared to be alone. They pulled a cot in and let people stay with me. Just knowing they were there was important. My mom and I spent every day together. Now, when I am frustrated, she lets me have those emotions, then she encourages me. My physical therapists were great. The doctors were great. It was really helpful that they kept me informed about everything. They were always honest with me."

Brannock's story shows us several things. Set goals, and then set milestones for yourself so that you can see tangible progress. "Now I make goals and check them off the list," Brannock said. "I ended up a few weeks ago getting on the floor, reading to my students with one on my lap."

Humor can be helpful. "I think for me, joking and laughter has really helped me heal. They helped me not take things so seriously. I think I use laughter and jokes for a lot of things even though there is a time to be serious and professional. I would make jokes right after my surgeries that I won't need pedicures."

Finally, after a traumatic event, a sense of closure is important. "Going back on the anniversary was important for me," Brannock said. "It was good to see the others again. I felt very lucky. Most importantly, I was able to see my mom finish the race and hug her. It completed the journey for me, seeing her cross the finish line."

WHY DO PEOPLE HELP OTHER PEOPLE? FOUNDATIONS OF COOPERATION AND SUPPORT

If you are to generate a network of social support, it will be useful to understand why people might be willing to provide assistance. This will help you construct your interpersonal support system.

Mathematical biologist Martin Nowak has identified five foundations of interpersonal reciprocity. What's most fascinating about his research is that it seems applicable not only to humans but to rudimentary biological systems such as colonies of yeast. According to Nowak, people will provide you assistance for one or more of these reasons:

1. *Direct reciprocity.* It's the principle of quid pro quo. I will help you now if you will help me at some later date.
2. *Spatial selection.* I will be more likely to help you if I know you via some mechanism of proximity. For example, we are neighbors, co-workers, attend the same gym, or participate in the same recreational activities.
3. *Genetic selection.* I am likely to help you if we are related.
4. *Indirect reciprocity (the most powerful).* I am likely to help you if you are seen as a desirable person to me, for example, you have a positive reputation, celebrity, or outstanding achievement.
5. *Group selection.* I am likely to help you if I'm altruistically inclined, or if I believe that helping you will be acting on behalf of the "greater good."

AVOID TOXIC PEOPLE

In this chapter we've emphasized the importance of interpersonal relations in resisting and bouncing back from adversity. The previous section provided suggestions on where to go for assistance. Now let's talk about where not to go.

It's important to understand that not all people are inclined to be of assistance in your time of need. In fact, some people may actually create problems for themselves and others. These folks can be toxic. Here, based on some of our own research and the research of others, is a list of people whose personalities make them toxic:

1. *Yes, But* personality (the excuse expert). These people are basically unhappy. They are so unhappy that they want to share their unhappiness (misery loves company). So they develop a passive-aggressive behavior style. Rather than being outwardly antagonistic, they are sarcastic with a smile. But most important, the Yes, But Personality interferes with progress (yours and its own) by having an excuse for every failure. When you offer a suggestion to assist after a Yes, But has solicited help from you, that person will say, "Yes, but . . ." and dismiss your suggestion. When you ask for help, you can also expect a "Yes, but . . ." followed by an excuse for not helping you.

2. *Entitled* personality ("It's all about me."). These people are very narcissistic. They will act as if the world revolves around them. An Entitled Personality has no room in its life for you or anyone else. Such people simply cannot be relied upon for support, unless there is something in it for them.

3. *Social Butterfly* personality (cultivates superficial relationships). These folks measure their worth by how many people they know and how many names they can drop. Social Butterflies are always cultivating relationships, albeit superficial ones. They must be the center of attention. They often act in dramatic and seductive ways. They seem incapable of meaningful reciprocal relationships.

4. *Aggressive* personality ("What's mine is mine; what's yours is mine. It's a jungle out there."). These people are simply aggressive. They do not honor interpersonal limits. They expect you to give to them without reciprocity. They demand it.

5. *Meticulous Me* personality ("Rules are rules."). These are rigid, obsessive, and compulsive people. They are disinclined to ask for help. They are less inclined to provide help. If you have a problem, it's probably because you deserve it, they would say. You need help? Help yourself!

6. *Frienemy* personality (hates your success). The frienemy is nice to your face but nasty behind your back. Such people are happy to help you, but only if they're doing far better than you. When frienemies do help, it's only to a point where you are still less successful than they are.

RX: PRESCRIPTIONS FOR BUILDING INTERPERSONAL SUPPORT

Here are some suggestions on how to build supportive relationships.

Rx 1: Homophily × Proximity

Begin to seek out and develop sources of social and professional support. The formula for doing so is quite simple: homophily × proximity. Said more simply, first identify individuals whom you believe are likely to share attitudes and values of compassion and mutual support (homophily). Then frequent places where you are likely to encounter such people. Go there on a regular basis (proximity). Proximity is the best predictor of relationship formation.

Find role models. Observe and learn from families, groups, organizations, and communities that seem most cohesive and intrinsically supportive. You'll find they share certain behaviors, such as frequent communications, formation, and practice of rituals (birthdays, anniversaries, etc.).

Seek out altruistic mentors—people who have a personal investment in your success or happiness. Their support should be unconditional. When they criticize, it must be done privately and constructively. They're never intentionally hurtful. In order to attract such support, you must earn friendships.

Rx 2: Show Appreciation

If you want to be appreciated, show appreciation. As philosopher and psychologist William James said, "The deepest craving of human nature is the desire to be appreciated." Here are some guidelines for how to best show appreciation:

* Regarding children, provide safety and compassionate guidance.

- To the elderly, show respect and gratitude.
- Regarding your employer, earn your income.
- To those who rely on you, provide presence and unwavering support.
- To a friend, show loyalty.
- To your spouse, show honor and fidelity.

In summary, work hard and be nice.

As Max Erhmann wrote in his 1927 classic prose poem *Desiderata*, "As far as possible without surrender be on good terms with all persons. Speak your truth quietly and clearly; and listen to others, even the dull and the ignorant; they too have their story. Avoid loud and aggressive persons, they are vexations to the spirit."

Rx 3: Be Patient

Control impulsive urges. Be patient with yourself and others. As Erika Brannock said, "I had been patient with two-year-olds. Now I had to be patient with myself."

Rx 4: Hanlon's Razor

Don't forget Hanlon's Razor: Never attribute to malice that which can be adequately explained by stupidity. In other words, don't take things personally. People really are inconsiderate at times and it has nothing to do with you.

Rx 5: Listen to Others, Especially Before You Speak

When we think of people who possess extraordinary interpersonal skill, we find they are good listeners. In even the briefest of encounters, they can make you feel important.

According to author Denise Restauri, charismatic people are good listeners who make the conversation about the other person. They show genuine interest. They let the world revolve around the other person. They remember the other person's name—and they use it. Case in point, Bill Clinton. Politics aside, Clinton is a master at making others feel special. According to blogger and self-described "World Changer" Matt McWilliams:

> Like him or not, Bill Clinton had a special gift. He was renowned for his ability to make people feel special. He had a unique ability to make one person in a room of 500 feel like the only one who mattered. And then he would make the next person feel the same way . . . and the next . . . and the next. He knew something that few people know: People don't want to be treated well. They want to be treated like they are the only one who matters.

So when you listen to people, truly listen. Look at the other person with interest. Do not multitask. Any time you have to say, "Go ahead, I'm listening," you're really not.

Rx 6: Practice the WAIT Principle

WAIT is an acronym for Why Am I Talking? Pause before you speak. Most important, ask yourself two questions: (1) Where are my words likely to direct the conversation? and (2) How would I feel if someone said that to me?

Rx 7: The Power of the Paraphrase

Perhaps the best single technique to convey effective listening requires you to be an active listener. When someone has finished making a point, use that person's name and then paraphrase in your words the essence of what you understood that person to say. Then ask a follow-up question. For example:

> MARTHA: I've been offered a new job. It could be a great opportunity, but it requires me to start all over in a new city. I'm in kind of a dilemma.
>
> YOU: Congratulations on the offer, Martha! It sounds like a tough decision. What are your thoughts so far?

Notice that it was a selfless response; you did not solve her problem for her. You did not share a similar experience. In essence, you kept the focus on her. You made her feel important because you asked her to tell you more. The more she hears herself speak out loud about the decision, the more likely she will solve it herself.

If nothing else, you may prosper from the naturally beneficial process of letting someone cathartically vent.

HOMEWORK

Pick one thing you can do, starting next Monday, that will help you develop networks of social and professional support. Write it here:

_____

_____

_____

Now send yourself an email as a reminder.

BUILDING COMMUNITY RESILIENCE

This book has focused on five factors of personal resilience, attributes we believe you need in order to achieve extraordinary success. The final factor reviewed was social support. Research suggests that it may be the single most important factor of those we have reviewed.

That having been said, this volume would not be complete without mention of resilience in communities, organizations, even nations. The adage "A rising tide lifts all boats" suggests that there may be factors that foster the resilience not only of individuals but individuals in the aggregate. The value of such an approach can be found in Aristotle's notion of synergy: "The whole is greater than the sum of its parts." That is certainly a core belief underlying the approach to resilience embraced by Navy SEALs.

We, the authors, have spent a lot of time during our careers observing tragedy on a community level. We have seen and assisted firsthand as villages (Coldenham, NY), organizations (Goldman Sachs, the New York City Police Department, the Oklahoma City Fire Department), communities (Oklahoma City, New Orleans, New York City), and even nations (Kuwait) bounce back from adversity. The goal of community resilience is to create a community culture that is characterized by robustness, adaptability, and the capacity for long-term sustainability, as well as recovery from adversity. The community culture of resilience is an environment where adaptability and resilience are not only fostered but are the core fabric of the culture itself. It's one with an atmosphere or climate where growth is promoted, support is abundant, and crisis is viewed as an opportunity.

Psychologist Ellen S. Zinner, along with social worker, author, and researcher Mary Beth Williams, analyzed community resilience in the wake of trauma and disaster in their 1998 book, *When a Community Weeps: Case Studies in Group Survivorship.* In it they reviewed noteworthy tragedies such as the 1986 space shuttle *Challenger* explosion; the 1994 sinking of a ferry, the *Estonia,* in the Baltic Sea; the 1995 terrorist bombing in Oklahoma City; the 1988 Armenian earthquake; and recurrent community violence. They conclude that community resilience is facilitated by six critical factors:

1. Connectedness of the members of the community
2. A cohesiveness and sense of belonging the members feel (group identity)
3. The rapidity of psychological intervention postevent
4. The degree of open, honest, and accurate communications
5. Ritualization where respect is shown to those who were lost and acknowledgment made to those who survived and especially to the "heroes"
6. Leadership

REBUILDING THE NATION OF KUWAIT

The nation of Kuwait lies in a portion of the Arabian Peninsula long known for its prominence as a commercial center and inhabited by a commercially oriented people. Kuwait possesses one of two significant natural harbors on the Arabian Gulf, thus making the area an ideal commercial center. Kuwait had a booming pearl trade and a prosperous freshwater transportation industry. It shipped Arabian horses all over the world. By the mid-18th century, the nation was well established as an economic and cultural hub.

In 1700, Sabah I had emerged as the sheikh of Kuwait, which was considered the Marseilles of the Arabian Gulf. Later, because of conflicts with Britain and neighboring Saudi Arabia, Kuwait fell into economic ruin. However, by the turn of the 20th century, oil had been discovered in the Middle East. In 1938, a major oil strike had been achieved in the Burgan region of Kuwait. In 1946, Kuwait inaugurated its first oil exportation. Economic ruin turned into seemingly boundless prosperity.

In 1981, the Arab Gulf Cooperation Council—consisting of Kuwait, Bahrain, Oman, Qatar, Saudi Arabia, and the United Arab Emirates—was formed to facilitate cooperation among major regional oil-producing countries. On July 17, 1990, Saddam Hussein, president of Iraq, which had also become a major oil-producing nation, accused Kuwait of driving down oil prices through overproduction.

On August 2, 1990, the Iraqi army invaded Kuwait, occupying the capital, Kuwait City, as well as the major petroleum-related facilities. The occupation was especially brutal. The Iraqis attempted to destroy any evidence of Kuwait's culture and identity. They sought a complete assimilation of the people of Kuwait into the Iraqi culture.

On January 16, 1991, military forces from a coalition of 34 nations led by the United States began an air war, and subsequently a ground campaign, designed to drive Iraqi forces from Kuwait. February 26, 2011, marked the 20th anniversary of the liberation of Kuwait from invading Iraqi forces.

In April 1992, the Amir of Kuwait, His Highness Sheikh Jaber Al-Ahmed Al-Sabah, created the Social Development Office (SDO) within the Amiri Diwan (the Office of His Highness the Amir of Kuwait) to preserve and rebuild Kuwait's "national identity." Under the leadership of its chairman, Basheer Al-Rashidi, the SDO had as one objective to foster national resilience and re-engender national cohesion. In 1992 the first author of this book was asked to serve in the SDO, and he was later appointed senior adviser on research to Amiri Diwan (Office of His Highness the Amir), in order to assist in rebuilding Kuwait's mental-health system.

What transpired in Kuwait over the next eight years was an approach to community resilience that closely followed the observations of Zinner and Williams:

- In order to foster the connectedness of the members of the community, the SDO was established with its mission to foster national resilience.

- In order to promote cohesiveness, a sense of belonging, and a national identity, numerous national celebrations and conferences were held showcasing Kuwaiti heritage.

Experts from all over the world were recruited to bring cutting-edge science and clinical interventions to Kuwait.

Open, honest, and accurate communications were facilitated, including opportunities at public forums for individuals to tell their stories of resilience as well as suffering.

National days of mourning as well as celebration were established. A special Martyr's Bureau was established to honor those lost in the war and to facilitate care of their families. National monuments were also erected.

The amir took a personal interest in the SDO and the Martyr's Bureau, housing them within his personal office. Members of his family were involved in the day-to-day operations of these offices. Leadership was highly visible, active, and personally invested.

Leadership is critical in the recovery of a community in the wake of adversity. Fortunately most communities do not suffer large-scale disasters, but they suffer adversity nevertheless. Leadership remains an essential aspect of recovery and community continuity.

MARTIN J. O'MALLEY, GOVERNOR OF MARYLAND

Born in 1963, Martin J. O'Malley was the 61st governor of Maryland. Throughout his career, he has shown the ability to offer resilience-based leadership.

O'Malley first served in elected office as a member of the Baltimore City Council. He was elected mayor of Baltimore in 1999, at a most challenging time for a city on the brink of social and economic implosion, and served until 2007. In 2002, *Esquire* magazine named O'Malley "The Best Young Mayor in the Country," and in 2005, *Time* magazine named him one of America's "Top 5 Big City Mayors." In 2006, he ran for governor and was elected, serving from 2007 to 2014, stepping down because of term limitations for governor. *Governing* magazine named him "Public Official of the Year" in 2009, and he was the chair of the Democratic Governors Association from 2011 to 2013.

O'Malley's 2013 legislative successes were described in a *Baltimore Sun* editorial as "without many parallels in recent Maryland history." Further, according to the *Sun:*

> Mr. O'Malley has demonstrated . . . leadership skills. When he was first elected mayor in 1999, the former two-term city councilman inherited a city of rising crime, failing schools and shrinking economic prospects. He was able to reverse course in all these areas.

O'Malley has undeniably made a difference in his state. According to a 2014 article in the *Huffington Post*, in the wake of O'Malley's tenure, Maryland had the fastest rate of job growth in the region, the #1 ranking for best public schools in America for an unprecedented five years in a row, the #1 ranking for holding down the cost of college tuition, and the #1 ranking for innovation and entrepreneurship for three years running.

You might think that in order to garner such accolades, O'Malley did what politicians are often accused of: talking a lot but doing little, and certainly not making waves. Hardly. For O'Malley, resilience involves having the courage to make difficult decisions that will further the greater good. And it means stepping up and taking responsibility for those decisions.

Reminiscent of Franklin Roosevelt's first term as president, when he faced a financial crisis that threatened all Americans, O'Malley, in his first year as governor, called a special session of the General Assembly to address a projected budget deficit for 2008–2009. He supported an unpopular tax increase because it would ultimately help all Marylanders.

In subsequent years, he courageously supported myriad controversial measures. Keep in mind, throughout this book we have shown that emerging from the abyss often means swimming against the tide. O'Malley vigorously lobbied for the installation of speed cameras, certainly unpopular among drivers. Although O'Malley endorsed tougher enforcement of immigration laws by the federal government, he signed into law a bill that would make the children of undocumented immigrants eligible for in-state college tuition under certain conditions. An Irish Catholic, O'Malley endorsed and signed into law a bill allowing same-sex marriages.

All of O'Malley's difficult decisions were subsequently supported by public referendum. They were seen, albeit sometimes painfully, as in the best interest of the community as a whole.

O'Malley's story of resilience is about more than having the courage to make difficult, often seemingly unpopular, decisions. It's also about the resilience of a community. Resilience is about people working together for the greater good. It's about people supporting people.

O'Malley described the lowest point in his career as a tragic firebombing in Baltimore when he was mayor. Reportedly as revenge for repeatedly calling police on suspected drug dealers, the home of a family named Dawson was bombed. Five children and their parents died.

How do you deal with that kind of tragedy when it happens on your watch? O'Malley told us closure is important as is beginning anew: "Adversity must be the beginning for change. I would not let tragedy be the final word." The perpetrator was convicted and given a life sentence without possibility of parole. The site of the Dawsons' home was reconstructed as the Dawson Safe Haven Community Center.

Looking back, O'Malley said, "There is strength in the spirit of a united people. They find a way to make sense of loss or defeat and to move forward. They find a way to rise above adversity."

What should we learn from O'Malley's story? In his own words: "The progress of a people is often in response to adversity. We are a stronger people united than we are divided. Resilience in the face of adversity gave our nation its birth. Resilience saved this republic in its darkest hours."

As for the glue that holds a people, a community, a nation, together, it is trust; and trust is based on truthfulness. "It is possible to move forward as a community only with trust," O'Malley said. "Be truthful about situations. For a community to bounce back, there must be honesty."

When asked what keeps him going through tough times, O'Malley responded, "My love for my children and the world they will inherit."

CHAPTER 6

LESSONS LEARNED ABOUT HUMAN RESILIENCE

The authors' quest to understand human resilience began as three very different journeys stretching over the course of almost 140 years of collective experience. One journey was that of a researcher and clinician seeking the "truth" to make others *stronger.* One journey was that of a successful entrepreneur, philanthropist, and grieving father seeking to help others so that they would never have to grieve as he did. The third was the journey of a U.S. Navy SEAL as part of a commitment to his SEAL brothers that began in Basic Underwater Demolition/SEAL (BUD/S) training.

But a fourth journey was soon to be revealed—our collective journey. One in which we analyzed our respective experiences for common elements while seeking to understand divergences. At the same time, we sought to integrate the perspectives of others, those we referred to as extraordinary people, all of whom had extraordinary stories of resilience in the face of extreme challenges, adversity, or even despair. Some enjoy varying degrees of celebrity, such as Cal Ripken Jr., Jim Craig, Ben Carson, Martin O'Malley, and Dutch Ruppersberger, but most do not. Whether the message was how to prepare for, endure, or rebound from adversity, the stories were replete with lessons to be learned. Could you see how these stories might help you in your own personal journey?

Our four respective journeys have not ended here. We're simply pausing to reflect and share. So, what do we think are the most significant lessons learned about human resilience as taught through history, personal reflection, scientific inquiry, and case study empiricism? What are the most important things we should teach our children to prepare them for a world that will not care for them as we would? What are the most important things we should teach aspiring athletes who desire to break the records of the past, the fledgling performers who aspire to bring us to our feet in spontaneous applause, and the students whose search for knowledge is not merely an academic pursuit but a passion? What is it we would teach the researchers who dream of curing cancer, the visionaries in business and finance who want to develop more efficient and effective organizations, those in leadership who understand that their legacy will reside not in what they take, but in what they leave to those who followed, and to the parents who understand that success in childrearing is defined as eventually seeing their role of parent in their children's lives become obsolete?

The answer we believe is to learn to be resilient in the wake of adversity, rejection, unfairness, and failure. Develop your own variation of psychological body armor derived from the five factors of human resilience discussed within this book. But as you consider how these five factors are applicable to your own life, here are a few things to keep in mind.

1. SIMPLICITY MATTERS

It is our collective opinion that the essence of human resilience resides in the five factors we have presented in this volume. When we initially published our findings in a professional journal, we identified seven characteristics of highly resilient people:

1. Optimism
2. Decisive action
3. Honesty
4. Tenacity
5. Interpersonal connectedness
6. Self-control
7. *Présence d'esprit*: calm, innovative, nondogmatic thinking

In *Stronger,* we have focused on the first five, our five factors of personal resilience, as major chapters while integrating aspects of self-control and nondogmatic thinking throughout those chapters simply for ease of presentation. That is not to diminish the respective values of the last two.

The science of human resilience can be paralyzingly granular and abstruse. Our quest was not intended to be definitive but to offer a user-friendly, heuristic, and prescriptive formulation.

2. OUR FIVE FACTORS ARE SEQUENTIAL

Ideally, our five factors of personal resilience are a sequential prescription:

1. *Active Optimism.* Active optimism is more than a hope or a belief. It's a *mandate* to bounce back, to be successful, to avoid being a victim. Active optimism is the belief that you can be an agent of change. Optimism breeds self-confidence that can become a self-fulfilling prophecy when it is honed with a dose of realism. Optimistic people are often viewed as more attractive to others than are pessimists. But the optimistic mandate to be resilient alone is not enough. It must lead to . . .

2. *Decisive Action.* You must act in order to rebound. You must learn to leave behind the comfort of the status quo and make difficult decisions. To paraphrase Mark Twain, if all you do is sit on the right track and wait for something to happen, it will. You will get run over. Or, perhaps at least an opportunity will be lost. Being decisive is hard. That's why it's rare. But by being decisive you distinguish yourself from others, usually in a positive way. As such you may then become the beneficiary of the *halo effect*, a lasting positive regard in the eyes of others. Making hard decisions to act is made easier when based upon a. . .

3. *Moral Compass.* There are four points to our moral compass: honor, integrity, fidelity, and ethics. Use them to guide your decisions under challenging circumstances. Simply do what is right and just. Your actions always have consequences. Consider the consequences of your actions not just

for you but for others as well. Once your decisions have been made, employ . . .

4. *Relentless Tenacity, Determination.* In 1989 Woody Allen was credited with proffering the notion that about 80 percent of success is showing up. We can modify that notion somewhat and say success often comes to those who not only show up but tenaciously show up. Show up and carry with you a relentless defiance of failure (but keep in mind that success may have to be redefined occasionally). Marine General Oliver Smith is quoted in *Time* magazine about his change of direction during the Korean War's Battle of Chosin Reservoir. He said, "Retreat, hell! We're not retreating, we're just advancing in a different direction." To find hidden opportunities and aid in physical and psychological energy, rely upon . . .

5. *Interpersonal Support.* Remember, no person is, nor ever should be, an island. Great strength is derived from the support of others. Going through life alone means no one has your back. Surround yourself with those of a compassionate heart and supportive presence. Knowing when to rely upon others is a sign of strength and wisdom. Supportive relationships are most commonly earned, however. Give to others. Be supportive without any expectation of a return. It will be the best external investment you can ever make.

3. RESILIENCE CAN BE LEARNED AT ANY AGE

Of course, we acknowledge that some things are best learned at a young age. This is because of the enhanced neural plasticity, or malleability, of the young brain. Ironically, according to new research, extreme adversity, stress, and traumatic events can cause the release of a cascade of neurological and neuroendocrine events that mimic, if not temporarily replicate, the neural plasticity of youth and in doing so actually facilitate learning.

The stress-related neurotransmitters norepinephrine and glutamate, as well as the N-methyl-D-aspartate (NMDA) receptor, a glutamate neurotransmitter receptor, are the predominant devices for controlling neuronal synaptic plasticity, which is the cellular basis for memory formation and memory function. Norepinephrine and NMDA are known to enhance memory under highly stressful conditions. Sometimes that's a good thing, sometimes it's not. A key phenomenological characteristic of many life-changing events is the fact that the memories of those events are easily recalled, often in vivid detail. They reside for a lifetime just beneath consciousness, ready to surface at a moment's notice. During our extensive work at Ground Zero after the 9/11 attacks, we were struck by the fact that the memories of that day were seared into the minds of those who were there, seemingly immune to the usual memory-degradation process.

On a more positive note, the first author still remembers the nurse who aided me after an unexpected surgery in a hospital away from home. I was afraid. She brought me ice cream. I proposed. She declined, citing an age disparity. I was 5, she was 28. I still remember her face.

Resilience is often about focusing on the positive aspects of life-changing events while minimizing the negative. Some argue that life-changing events that seem horrific at first later become a platform for subsequent growth and new opportunities.

4. SELF-EFFICACY IS A USEFUL FRAMEWORK BY WHICH TO LEARN EACH OF THE FIVE FACTORS OF HUMAN RESILIENCE

Albert Bandura's brilliant model for acquiring self-efficacy and personal agency (the optimistic belief that you can be an effective agent of change) is a useful tool for learning each of our five factors of human resilience. So let's review. Bandura offers four learning prescriptions for the acquisition and maintenance of self-efficacy that are generically applicable to *each* of our five factors of personal resilience:

1. Seek to successfully demonstrate and repeatedly practice each of our five factors of personal resilience. Success is a powerful learning tool—Just do it! If the challenge is too large or complex at first, start by taking small steps in the desired direction. Don't try to achieve too much at first. And keep trying until you succeed. The first success is the hardest.

2. Observe resilient people. Use them as role models. Human beings learn largely by observation. Frequent venues where you can watch people exhibiting the skills you wish to acquire. Read books about people who have overcome obstacles similar to those you face. Call or write them. Ask them to share their lessons learned. Their successes will be contagious.

3. Vigorously pursue the encouragement and support of others. Affiliate with supportive and compassionate people who are willing to give of themselves to be supportive of you.

4. Practice self-control. In highly stressful times, myriad physiological and behavioral reactions occur. Physiologically,
people experience the fight-or-flight response we mentioned in Chapter One. This cascade of hormones such as
adrenalin better prepares you to fight or to flee a threat.
They increase your heart rate, muscle strength, and tension. They dramatically improve your memory for certain
things while decreasing your ability to remember others,
and they cause your blood vessels to shift their priorities.
This often results in headaches, cold hands and feet, and
even an upset gastrointestinal system. The most significant
problem, however, is that this very basic survival mechanism also tends to interfere with rational judgment and
problem solving.

According to Bandura's research, during times such as these,
it's important to control your stress arousal so it doesn't become
excessive. Techniques such as breath counting or controlled deep
breathing (used by snipers in the military), distraction techniques,
and visual imagery have all been shown to be effective in reducing
excessive stress arousal.

People often act impulsively in reaction to stressful events,
sometimes running away from them. Remember the 1999 movie
Runaway Bride, starring Richard Gere and Julia Roberts? It was
the fictional story of a woman who had a penchant for falling in
love and getting engaged, then developing cold feet and leaving
her fiancés at the altars. On a more somber note, after the conclu-
sion of the Vietnam War, many veterans chose to retreat to lives of
isolation and solitude. The stress of war and the lack of social support motivated many to simply withdraw from society.

Similarly, over many years of clinical practice, we have seen individuals who have great difficulty establishing meaningful relationships after surviving a traumatic or vitriolic divorce. It's hard for them to trust another person after having been "betrayed." They exhibit approach-avoidance behaviors—engaging in a relationship initially but backing away when it intensifies.

Contrary to these patterns of escape and avoidance, sometimes people will impulsively act aggressively in response to stressful situations. Chronic irritability is often an early warning sign of subsequent escalating aggressive behavior. Rarely, although sometimes catastrophically, people will choose to lie, cheat, or steal in highly stressful situations. For years, psychologists have tried to predict dishonesty using psychological testing. The results have been uninspiring. The reason is that the best predictor of dishonesty is finding oneself in a highly stressful situation. So in highly stressful times, resist the impulsive urges to take the easy way out.

Also, remember to take care of yourself, physically as well as psychologically. Maladaptive self-medication is a common pattern of behavior for people who find themselves in the abyss. Alcohol has long been observed as a chemical crutch. Others that have only recently emerged are the myriad energy drinks on the market. Both of these crutches have been linked to numerous physical ailments and even deaths. If you are looking for the best single physical mechanism to aid you in your ascent from the abyss, it's establishing healthy patterns of rest and sleep.

5. IT'S IMPORTANT TO MONITOR YOUR RESILIENCE

In Chapters One through Five, we asked you to complete self-assessments so you might gain some insight into your resilience.

These were not direct clinical assessments but subjective surveys that allow you to quickly and easily assess your resilience on an ongoing basis. You can use these simple tools to plot the trajectory of your resilience over time.

For example, take these surveys the first of every month and see how these indirect measures of resilience vary with time. Should you see a decline, look for the cause. Ask yourself if there is something you can do to reduce or eliminate exposure to stressful events. If not, make a concerted effort to employ the tactics in this book to strengthen your personal resilience.

While these surveys are not clinical assessments per se, we do know that the factors of resilience they measure inversely correlate with stress arousal and burnout. Simply said, it appears that the greater the resilience factors in your life, the less stress and burnout you'll experience. So work these techniques and take the assessments monthly. The higher your scores, the better.

6. STUDY THE PAST: RESILIENCE IN THEIR OWN WORDS

Those who went before us can teach us a great deal. As philosopher and author George Santayana wrote, "Those who cannot remember the past are condemned to repeat it." George S. Everly Sr., whom we profiled in Chapter Three, was a member of Tom Brokaw's "greatest generation." A musician for 80 years, he once said, "Old musicians never die; their song has ended, but their melody lingers on." Extraordinarily resilient people leave a melody that lingers. It's a melody that can teach us much if we are wise enough to listen. Let's listen one last time.

On Active Optimism

Resilience begins with a belief. It can be a belief about yourself, or about how the things will turn out.

Abbey-Robin Tillery, Ph.D., psychologist "Finding a way to imagine a better life for oneself is the first step in making it happen; telling people to never give up does not last if people can't even imagine a better life. Believe in yourself. Believe you are destined for something better. There is a strong intuitive sense in us all that screams out against all odds, 'I will make it!'"

Jim Craig, goalkeeper, 1980 Olympic "Miracle on Ice" "My life in my small way is to help make people believe and dream while appreciating what they have. To me life is not what you take, but what you give, and how you share what you have learned . . . from your mistakes as well as your victories." Craig's legacy is more than an unlikely Olympic gold medal. It's the reminder to both the dreamer and the underdog that miracles can happen. "Do you believe in miracles?"

On Decisiveness

Being decisive takes courage. It often means defying conventional wisdom and practice.

Ben Carson, MD, Johns Hopkins University neurosurgeon Ben Carson's message is one of self-determination. "What happens with your life is up to you," he said. "Growing up, when I read books about successful people, I found out that many didn't start out that way. I began to understand it's not the environment. It's you and your attitude. You can work hard and achieve whatever you want.

"I ignored the pessimists from the time I was a teenager throughout my entire career. My adviser wanted me to drop out of medical school. When I started performing surgical procedures that others had failed to perform or that had never been tried before, people said, 'You can't do that.' Because of our successes, those procedures are now being done routinely all over the world. If you use intellect then you can learn from what has happened in the past and from what others are doing, and then you can move much faster."

When asked to summarize his concept of resilience, Carson told us: When adversity strikes, simply refuse to be a victim.

On Using a Moral Compass

Dutch Ruppersberger, U.S. congressman "Just do the right thing and everything else will take care of itself. Make your legacy tenacity and integrity. When you get knocked down, get up. . . . You want to be respected for who you are and what you've done. In the final analysis, your legacy will be your deeds, not your words."

George S. Everly Sr., soldier, husband, father, and member of the greatest generation A child of the Great Depression, Everly learned that survival was a "team sport." Raised on a farm without running water or electricity, he learned how important it was to play his role and play it well, without asking, "What's in it for me?" After enlisting in the U.S. Army, he went to war, during which his early lessons on interdependence were reinforced. He learned that there is no such thing as "an army of one." After coming home from war, he sacrificed a career in Hollywood playing in the movies with the "big bands" of the era so that he could create a more stable environment in which to raise a family. He later ended a successful career in finance prematurely in order to better care for his spouse, who suffered from a chronic illness.

Once, at an airport, Everly noticed that a man in the food line behind him was wearing a U.S. Army uniform. When Everly paid for his own food, he asked the cashier to also charge the soldier's food to his credit card. The soldier seemed shocked. When asked why he paid for the soldier's food, Everly said, "A lot of my friends died defending this country in World War II. Soldiers are willing to go to war and die for us now. They don't ask for anything in return. The least we can do is show them a little respect and say thank you when we can."

On Tenacity

Patrick Rummerfield, accident survivor Patrick Rummerfield was given 72 hours to live after a terrible car crash. Having beaten those odds, but as a quadriplegic, he was sent to a nursing home to slowly die over the course of four or five years.

As living testament to the fact that success begets success, he noticed his big toe move in response to thinking about driving a race car. Against his physician's advice, he entered intensive rehabilitation. Over the course of 17 years, he recovered the use of his arms and legs and has run a marathon. Rummerfield said while at dinner one night, "No one can predict the future. Where there is life there is hope. Where there is hope there can be tenacity. Where there is tenacity all things are possible."

Cal Ripken Jr., Hall of Fame professional baseball player "In the face of adversity or in the wake of failure, rather than crumble, know that there is always light at the end of the tunnel and positives. When you are going through a tough period, you have to take some positives away from each challenge, and even failure, then persevere. Persevering builds strength and character that will serve you well at a later time."

Cal Ripken Jr. is that rare combination of extraordinary athlete, successful businessman, and philanthropist, but most of all he is a gentleman who has handled the pressures as well as the privileges of international celebrity with integrity, grace, and sublimity.

On Interpersonal Support

Erika Brannock, survivor of the Boston Marathon bombing As if taking Ben Carson's advice to heart, Erika Brannock refuses to be a victim. An act of terrorism took her leg, but not her will to survive and prosper. She exemplifies a flexibility in attitude that becomes a self-fulfilling prophecy and reminds us of the importance of the support of others at times of need.

"Yes, I lost my legs but I am still here. I can still do all that I did before. I just have to get used to doing them a different way. You have to choose to focus on the positive not the negative. I say to people, 'Don't refer to me as a victim.' If you have power and motivation then you can get through it. I think it's going to prove to me that down the road I can handle anything because I have been able to get through this."

Erika credits her mother, her students, and the supportive health professionals who cared for her as the key to her recovery.

Martin J. O'Malley, governor of Maryland No man is an island, according to John Donne. We are all connected. Resiliency is often a group project. "The progress of a people is often in response to adversity. We are a stronger people united than we are divided. Resilience in the face of adversity gave our nation its birth. Resilience saved this republic in its darkest hours."

Speaking of the self-fulfilling prophecy, never forget the words of the Brazilian writer and journalist Fernando Sabino: "In the end everything will be OK. If it's not OK, then it is not yet the end."

REFERENCES

PREFACE

Gibbs, Nancy, and Mark Thompson. "The War on Suicide?" TIME.com, July 23, 2012. Accessed July 12, 2014. http://content.time.com/time/magazine/article/0,9171,2119337,00.html.

CHAPTER 1: ACTIVE OPTIMISM AND THE SELF-FULFILLING PROPHECY

Peterson, Christopher. *A Primer in Positive Psychology*. New York: Oxford, 2006.

Everly, George S., Jr., and Jeffrey M. Lating. *Clinical Guide to the Treatment of the Human Stress Response*. 3rd ed. New York: Pearson, 2013.

Everly, George S., Jr. *Fostering Human Resilience*. 2nd ed. Ellicott City, MD: Chevron, 2013.

Everly, George S., Jr., Douglas A. Strouse, and George S. Everly III. *The Secrets of Resilient Leadership*. New York: DiaMedica, 2010.

Cannon, Walter B. "The Emergency Function of the Adrenal Medulla in Pain and in the Major Emotions." *American Journal of Physiology* 33 (1914): 356–372.

Everly, George S., Jr., and Herbert Benson. "Disorders of Arousal and the Relaxation Response." *International Journal of Psychosomatics* 36 (1989): 15–22.

Gellhorn, Ernst. "Central Nervous System Tuning and Its Implications for Neuropsychiatry." *Journal of Nervous and Mental Disease* 147 (1968): 148–162.

Gellhorn, Ernst. "Further Studies on the Physiology and Pathophysiology of the Tuning of the Central Nervous System." *Psychosomatics* 10 (1969): 94–104.

Cannon, Walter B. *Wisdom of the Body*. New York: Norton, 1932.

Charney, Dennis S. "Psychobiological Mechanisms of Resilience and Vulnerability: Implications for Successful Adaptation to Extreme Stress." *American Journal of Psychiatry* 161 (2004): 195–216.

Ahmed, Ayesha S. "Posttraumatic Stress Disorder, Resilience, and Vulnerability." *Advances in Psychiatric Treatment* 13 (2007): 369–375.

Morgan, Charles A., III, Sheila Wang, Steven M. Southwick, Ann Rasmusson, Gary Hazlett, Richard L. Hauger, and Dennis S. Charney. "Plasma Neuropeptide-Y Concentrations in Humans Exposed to Military Survival Training." *Biological Psychiatry* 47 (2000): 902–909.

Smith, Kenneth J., George S. Everly Jr., and Anthony Johns. "The Role of Cognitive-Affective Arousal in the Dynamics of Stressor-to-Illness Processes." *Contemporary Accounting Research* 9 (1993): 432–449.

Smith, Kenneth J., George S. Everly Jr., and G. Timothy Haight. "SAS4: Validation of a Four-Item Measure of Worry and Rumination." *Advances in Accounting Behavioral Research* 15 (2012): 101–131.

Sun Tzu. (translated by James Clavell). *The Art of War*. London: Hodder & Stoughton. (p. 113)

CHAPTER 2: THE COURAGE TO BE DECISIVE AND TAKE PERSONAL RESPONSIBILITY

Seligman, Martin E. P. *Learned Optimism*. New York: Vintage, 2006.

Seligman, Martin E. P. *Optimistic Child*. New York: Houghton Mifflin, 2007. (pp. 35, 40)

Neuharth, Al. *Confessions of an S.O.B.* New York: Doubleday, 1989.

Ripken, Cal, Jr. Speech at Camden Yards, Baltimore, MD, on unveiling of bronze sculptures of Oriole baseball players. September 6, 2012. Transcript available at *Baltimore Sun*, September 6.

Jordan, Michael. "Failure." Nike. 1997. Accessed June 1, 2104. www.youtube.com/watch?v=GuXZFQKKF7A.

University of York. "Why Do Rubber Balls Bounce?" Simple Science Webpage, 2012. Accessed April 14, 2014. www.york.ac.uk/media/cll/documents/rubberbounce.pdf.

Burd, Nicholas A., Daniel W. D. West, Aaron W. Staples, Philip J. Atherton, Jeff M. Baker, Daniel R. Moore, Andrew M. Holwerda, Gianni Parise, Michael J. Rennie, Steven K. Baker, Stuart M. Phillips. "Low-Load High Volume Resistance Exercise Stimulates Muscle Protein Synthesis More Than High-Load Low Volume Resistance Exercise in Young Men." *PLoS ONE* 5, no. 8 (Aug. 9, 2010): e12033. Accessed May 20, 2014. doi:10.1371/journal.pone.0012033.

Smith, Kenneth J., George S. Everly Jr., and G. Timothy Haight. "SAS4: Validation of a Four-Item Measure of Worry and Rumination." *Advances in Accounting Behavioral Research* 15 (2012): 101–131.

Everly, George S., Jr., Jeanette A. Davey, Kenneth J. Smith, Jeffrey M. Lating, and Frederick C. Nucifora. "A Defining Aspect of Human Resilience in the Workplace: A Structural Modeling Analysis." *Disaster Medicine and Public Health Preparedness* 5 (2011): 98–105.

U.S. Department of Labor. *Business Dynamics Statistics*. Washington, DC: Bureau of Labor Statistics, 2009.

Everly, George S., Jr., Douglas A. Strouse, and George S. Everly III. *The Secrets of Resilient Leadership*. New York: DiaMedica, 2010.

Everly, George S., Jr., and Jeffrey M. Lating. *Clinical Guide to the Treatment of the Human Stress Response*. 3rd ed. New York: Pearson, 2013.

Sanderson, William C., Ronald M. Rapee, and David H. Barlow. "The Influence of an Illusion of Control on Panic Attacks Induced Via Inhalation of 5.5% Carbon Dioxide-Enriched Air." *Archives of General Psychiatry* 46 (1989): 157–162.

Craig, Jim, and Don Yaeger. *Gold Medal Strategies*. New York: Wiley, 2011.

Sun Tzu. (translated by James Clavell). *The Art of War*. London: Hodder & Stoughton.

U.S. Centers for Disease Control and Prevention. *Preventing Chronic Diseases: Investing Wisely in Health: Screening to Prevent Cancer Deaths*. Atlanta: Centers for Disease Control and Prevention, 2008.

David Drew Clinic. Accessed July 9, 2014. www.daviddrew.com.

Isaacson, Walter. *Steve Jobs*. New York: Simon and Schuster, 2012.

Langer, Ellen J., and Judith Rodin. "The Effects of Choice and Enhanced Personal Responsibility for the Aged: A Field Experiment in an Institutional Setting." *Journal of Personality and Social Psychology* 34, no. 2 (August 1976): 191–198.

Everly, George S., Jr., and Jeffrey M. Lating. *Personality Guided Therapy for Posttraumatic Stress Disorder*. Washington, DC: APA Press, 2004.

Bandura, Albert. *Self-Efficacy: The Exercise of Control*. New York: Freeman, 1997.

Peterson, Christopher. *A Primer in Positive Psychology*. New York: Oxford, 2006.

Thorndike, Edward L. "A Constant Error in Psychological Ratings." *Journal of Applied Psychology* 4, no. 1 (1920): 25–29. Accessed May 31, 2014. doi: 10.1037/h0071663.

Fremantle, Arthur. *Three Months in the Southern States*. New York: Bradburn, 1864.

Griessman, Gene. *The Words Lincoln Lived By*. New York: Fireside, 1997. (p. 98)

C-SPAN. C-Span Historians 2009 Historians Presidential Survey, 2009. www.c-span.org/presidentialsurvey

Gladwell, Malcolm. *Outliers: The Story of Success*. New York: Little, Brown, 2008.

Koretsky, Jennifer. "10 Benefits of Having Attention Deficit." Mental Health Matters. Accessed July 28, 2014. http://mental-health-matters.com/10-benefits-of-having-attention-deficit-disorder-add/.

Firestone, Rachel M., and George S. Everly Jr. "A Pilot Investigation in Constructing Crisis Communications: What Leads to Best Practice?" *International Journal of Emergency Mental Health* 15, no. 3 (2013): 159–164.

Lewin, Kurt, Ronald Lippit, and Ralph K. White. "Patterns of Aggressive Behavior in Experimentally Created Social Climates." *Journal of Social Psychology* 10 (1939): 271–301.

Gladwell, Malcolm. *What the Dog Saw*. New York: Little, Brown, 2009.

Ariew, Roger. *Ockham's Razor: A Historical and Philosophical Analysis of Ockham's Principle of Parsimony*. Champaign-Urbana: University of Illinois, 1976.

Pascal, Blaise. *Pascal's Pensees*. New York: Dutton, 1958.

CHAPTER 3: THE MORAL COMPASS: HONESTY, INTEGRITY, FIDELITY, AND ETHICAL BEHAVIOR

Twain, Mark. *Mark Twain in Eruption: Hitherto Unpublished Pages About Men and Events*. Edited by Bernard De Voto. New York: Harper & Brothers, 1940.

Wolf, Stewart, and John G. Bruhn. *The Power of Clan: The Influence of Human Relationships on Heart Disease*. London: Transaction, 1993.

Neal, Zachary P., and Jennifer Watling Neal. "The (In)compatibility of Diversity and Sense of Community." *American Journal of Community Psychology* 53, no. 1–2 (March 2014): 1–12. Accessed July 1, 2014. doi: 10.1007/s10464-013-9608-0.

Verducci, Tom. "To Cheat or Not to Cheat." *Sports Illustrated*, June 4, 2012. Accessed July 6, 2014. http://www.si.com/more-sports/2012/05/29/baseball-steroids.

ESPN.com. *Lance Armstrong: Singled Out*. Updated December 12, 2013. Accessed July 29, 2014. http://espn.go.com/sports/endurance/story/_/id/10124453/lance-armstrong-singled-nice.

Ellyatt, Holly. "Corruption Worsens Amid Deep Distrust of Government." CNBC.com, July 9, 2013. Accessed July 1, 2014. http://www.cnbc.com/id/100871669#.

Transparency International. Global Corruption Barometer 2013. Accessed July 6, 2014. http://www.transparency.org/whatwedo/pub/global_corruption_barometer_2013.

Randall, Willard Sterne. *Benedict Arnold: Patriot and Traitor*. New York: Dorset, 1990.

Martin, James Kirby. *Benedict Arnold: Revolutionary Hero (An American Warrior Reconsidered)*. New York: New York University Press, 1997.

Valentino-DeVries, Jennifer, and Siobhan Gorman. "What You Need to Know on New Details on NSA Spying." *Wall Street Journal*, August 20, 2013. Accessed June 28, 2014. http://online.wsj.com/articles/SB10001424127887324108204579025222244858490.

Griffin, Jennifer. "CIA Operators Were Denied Request for Help During Benghazi Attack." FoxNews.com, October 26, 2012. Accessed July 14, 2014. http://www.foxnews.com/politics/2012/10/26/cia-operators-were-denied-request-for-help-during-benghazi-attack-sources-say/.

Crombie, I. M. *An Examination of Plato's Doctrines*. London: Routledge & Kegan Paul, 1963.

Kelling, George L. and James Q. Wilson, "Broken Windows: The Police and Neighborhood Safety." *Atlantic Monthly* (March 1982): 29–38.

Sousa, William, and George Kelling. "Of 'Broken Windows.' Criminology, and Criminal Justice." In *Police Innovation: Contrasting Perspectives*, edited by David Weisburd and Anthony Braga, 77–97. New York: Cambridge University Press, 2006.

CHAPTER 4: RELENTLESS TENACITY: TRY, TRY AGAIN

Meacham, Jon. *Franklin and Winston: An Intimate Portrait of an Epic Friendship*. New York: Random House, 2003. (p. 53)

Ripken, Cal, Jr. *The Longest Season*. New York: Philomel, 2007.

Ripken, Cal, Jr., and Donald T. Phillips. *Get in the Game*. New York: Gotham, 2007.

CHAPTER 5: GAIN STRENGTH FROM THE SUPPORT OF OTHERS

Aristotle. *The Metaphysics*. Translated by H. Tredennick. Cambridge, MA: Harvard University Press, 1961.

Antonovsky, Aaron. *Health, Stress and Coping*. San Francisco: Jossey-Bass, 1979.

Berkowitz, Leonard. "Group Standards, Cohesiveness, and Productivity." *Human Relations* 7 (1954): 509–519.

Beal, Daniel J., Robin R. Cohen, Michael J. Burke, and Christy L. McLendon. "Cohesion and Performance in Groups: A Meta-Analytic Clarification of Construct Relation." *Journal of Applied Psychology* 88 (2003): 989–1004.

Axelrod, Robert, and William D. Hamilton. "The Evolution of Cooperation." *Science* 211, no. 4489 (March 27, 1981): 1390–1396.

Ozer, Emily, Suzanne Best, Tami Lipsey, and Daniel Weiss. "Predictors of Posttraumatic Stress Disorder and Symptoms in Adults: A Meta-Analysis." *Psychological Bulletin* 129, no. 1 (2003): 52–73.

Everly, George S., Jr., Douglas A. Strouse, and George S. Everly III. *The Secrets of Resilient Leadership*. New York: DiaMedica, 2010.

Nowak, Martin. "Five Rules for the Evolution of Cooperation." *Science* 314 (Nov. 8, 2006): 1560–1563.

Henry, James P., and Patricia M. Stephens. *Stress, Health, and the Social Environment*. New York: Springer, 1977.

Lynch, James J. *The Broken Heart: The Medical Consequences of Loneliness*. New York: Basic Books, 1977.

Cacioppo, John T., and William Patrick. *Loneliness*. New York: Norton, 2008.

Holt-Lunstad, Julianne, Timothy B. Smith, and J. Bradley Layton. "Social Relationships and Mortality Risk: A Meta-Analytic Review." *PloS Med* 7, no. 7 (July 27, 2010): e1000316. Accessed May 31, 2014. doi: 10.1371.

Wolf, Stewart, and John G. Bruhn. *The Power of Clan: The Influence of Human Relationships on Heart Disease*. London: Transaction, 1993. (pp. 78, 122)

Berne, Eric. *Games People Play—The Basic Handbook of Transactional Analysis*. New York: Ballantine, 1964.

Millon, Theodore, and George S. Everly Jr. *Personality and Its Disorders*. New York: Wiley, 1985.

Frank, Jerome D. "Therapeutic Factors in Psychotherapy. *Journal of Psychotherapy* 25 (1971): 350–361.

Zinner, Ellen, and Mary Beth Williams. *When a Community Weeps*. Philadelphia: Brunner Mazel, 1998.

Green, Erica. "Maryland Schools Rank No. 1 Fifth Year in a Row." *Baltimore Sun,* January 10, 2013. Accessed July 11, 2014. http://articles.baltimoresun.com/2013-01-10/news/bs-md-maryland-number-one-20130110_1_maryland-schools-rank-state-high-marks-superintendent-lillian-m-lowery.

CHAPTER 6: LESSONS LEARNED ABOUT HUMAN RESILIENCE

Everly, George S., Jr., Dennis K. McCormack, and Douglas A. Strouse. "Seven Characteristics of Highly Resilient People." *International Journal of Emergency Mental Health* 14, no. 2 (2012): 137–143.

Suzuki, Akinobu, Sheena A. Josselyn, Paul W. Frankland, Shoichi Masushige, Alcino J. Silva, and Satoshi Kida. "Memory Reconsolidation and Extinction Have Distinct Temporal and Biochemical Signatures." *Journal of Neuroscience*, 24, no. 20 (2004): 4787–4795.

Everly, George S., Jr., and Jeffrey M. Lating. *Personality Guided Therapy for Posttraumatic Stress Disorder*. Washington, DC: APA Press, 2004.

Everly, George S., Jr., and Jeffrey M. Lating. *Clinical Guide to the Treatment of the Human Stress Response*. 3rd ed. New York: Pearson, 2013.

Li, Fei, and Joe Z. Tsien. "Memory and the NMDA Receptors." *New England Journal of Medicine* 361, no. 3 (2009): 302–303.

Bandura, Albert. *Self-Efficacy: The Exercise of Control*. New York: Freeman, 1997.

Selye, Hans. *The Stress of Life*. New York: McGraw-Hill, 1956.

Santayana, George. *Life of Reason*. New York: Scribner, 1905. (p. 285)

INDEX

ABOUT THE AUTHORS

George Everly Jr., Ph.D., is one of the founding fathers of modern stress management and disaster mental health. He currently serves as Associate Professor of Psychiatry and Behavioral Sciences at the Johns Hopkins University School of Medicine, Professor of Psychology at Loyola University Maryland, and Executive Director of Resiliency at UMBC Training Centers. In addition, he serves on the faculties of the Johns Hopkins Public Health Preparedness Programs and the Department of International Health, both at the Johns Hopkins Bloomberg School of Public Health. Dr. Everly has served as a consultant to FEMA, the FBI National Academy, ATF, and US Federal Air Marshals, and was formerly Senior Research Advisor, Office of His Highness the Amir of Kuwait.

Trained in clinical psychology and neuropsychology, Dr. Everly is a Fellow of the American Psychological Association, a Fellow of the Academy of Psychosomatic Medicine, and is Board Certified by the American Psychological Association. He has held visiting or honorary professorships at the University of Hong Kong, Universidad de Flores Buenos Aires, and Universidad de Weiner Lima Peru. He has given invited lectures in twenty-two countries on six continents. Dr. Everly's biography appears in *Who's Who in America* and *Who's Who in the World*.

Douglas A. Strouse, Ph.D., is the Managing Partner of Wexley Consulting HRD, LLC, an international management consulting firm whose clients have included companies such as Duracell, Moen, Oldsmobile, Rubbermaid, United, Frito Lay, GE, General Motors, Goodyear, Corning, and many others. He is also the founder of Global Data Source

LLC, a national data management and services firm, and is founder and President of the Chief Executive Officers Club (CEO Club) of Baltimore, a nonprofit organization that provides an educational forum for executives of small and mid-size companies. He also helped launch the CEO Club chapters in the Philippines, Dubai, and Greece. In addition, Dr. Strouse serves on the Johns Hopkins Hospital Department of Psychiatry Advisory Board.

Dr. Strouse has extensive experience in creating organizational resilience for troubled businesses. He holds a master's degree in communications and received his doctoral degree in organizational management and organizational psychology. He has coauthored two books and written more than 110 professional articles, and has spoken extensively to various business groups throughout the United States.

Dennis K. McCormack, Ph.D., is one of the original Navy SEALs, and he pioneered SEAL combat doctrine and tactics in Vietnam. Dr. McCormack holds a bachelor's degree in mathematics; a master's degree in guidance and counseling; and doctoral degrees in leadership and human behavior as well as professional psychology. Serving as a supervisory psychologist for the Department of Defense (Army), he received official commendation for meritorious performance of duty for demonstrated professionalism and dedicated commitment to excellence as Chief, Department of Behavioral Medicine, Winn Army Community Hospital, Fort Stewart, Georgia. Dr. McCormack graduated from the Army Management Staff College, Sustaining Base Leadership program as well as the Leadership, Education, Awareness and Development (LEAD) program. He has taught and coached at the high school and university levels. His teaching at Armstrong Atlantic State University in Savannah, Georgia, included coursework on theory of counseling and psychotherapy; abnormal psychology; and clinical psychology. Dr. McCormack is a highly respected researcher on the topics of managing and thriving under stress.